San Franci

THE SUPER YEARS

San Francisco 49ers

THE SUPER YEARS

Photographs by Michael Zagaris

Profiles by Glenn Dickey

Chronicle Books ▪ San Francisco

Dedication

To Kristin and Ari, Nick and Dorothy Zagaris, for everything, and to Mr. D and Coach Walsh, with warmth, gratitude, and thanks.

Copyright 1989 by Chronicle Books.

Text Copyright © 1989 by Glenn Dickey.

Photographs Copyright © 1989 by Michael Zagaris.

Printed in Japan.

Library of Congress Cataloging in Publication Data

Dickey, Glenn.
   San Francisco 49ers: the super years / Glenn Dickey; photographs by Michael Zagaris.
   p.   cm.
   ISBN 0-87701-702-6
   1. San Francisco 49ers (Football team) — History. 2. Football players — United States — Biography. 3. San Francisco 49ers (Football team) — pictorial works. I. Zagaris, Michael. II .Title. III. Title: San Francisco Forty-niners.
GV956.S3D53 1989   89-15900
796.332'64'0979461 — dc20   CIP

Book and cover design: Nielsen/O'Brien

Produced in association with
Baron Wolman/SQUAREBOOKS

Distributed in Canada by
Raincoast Books
112 East 3rd Avenue
Vancouver, B.C. V5T 1C8

10 9 8 7 6 5 4 3 2 1

Chronicle Books
275 Fifth Street
San Francisco, California 94103

Captions for photographs in the Preface, Foreword, and Introduction are:

Page 2: December 19, 1983; Candlestick Park. Bill Walsh meets with Joe Montana late in the third quarter.

Page 5: July 1979; Kezar Stadium. In his first season, Bill Walsh brought the 49ers back to Kezar Stadium for one final scrimmage in late July 1979. Kezar had been the home of the 49ers since the team's beginning in 1946 but the team had not played there since the January 1971 Championship game loss to Dallas.

Page 7: Michael Zagaris, 1985. Photo by Kristin Sundbom.

Page 8: October 21, 1984; Astrodome, Houston. George Seifert makes defensive adjustments at halftime.

Page 11: January 10, 1982; NFC Championship game; Candlestick Park. The crowd erupts moments after "The Catch" sends the 49ers to their first Super Bowl.

Page 12: September 11, 1988; Meadowlands, New York. The defense stops the Giants.

Page 13: September 8, 1983; Minneapolis. In the narrow visitor's locker room, the 49ers prepare to meet the Vikings.

Page 14: October 30, 1988; Candlestick Park. The defense gangs up on the Vikings.

CONTENTS

PREFACE

It was mid-October of 1954 when my dad took my brother Bruce and me to see our first 49ers game. Ike was president, Cinemascope was the rage, the New York Giants had just swept the Cleveland Indians in the Series, and Fireman Frank was still a big happening on TV in San Francisco. That was all irrelevant on this particular Sunday.

The bright green of the grass appeared almost Day-Glo to my young eyes when we first walked through the tunnel and out into Kezar Stadium. That afternoon we were playing the Detroit Lions, and in those days the Lions and the Cleveland Browns were the perennial powers. The 49ers appeared first, streaming onto the field from the tunnel at the east end of the stadium. Though it was still an hour before kick-off, the stands were filling rapidly, and when the Lions took the field they were greeted by the raucous crowd with boos, hoots, and derisive yells. The game was a classic. The 49ers, led by Y.A. Tittle and Joe "The Jet" Perry, were resplendent in their bright red jerseys and helmets with white stripes and numerals. The Lions, attired in silver helmets and pants with Honolulu blue jerseys, were led by Bobby Layne and Doak Walker. The game went back and forth and late in the third quarter the fog rolled in; sea gulls dive-bombed the crowd, crapping on fans and occasionally battling each other. The booze flowed freely in those days at Kezar. In the end, Hugh "The King" McElheney hotfooted through Buddy Parker's boys like a shoplifter through Macy's on Christmas Eve and we prevailed 37-31. We filed out of Kezar hoarse and exhausted. I was hooked for life. Forget Rocky Marciano, forget Quo Vadis and the Knights of the Round Table. *This* was the real thing.

As the years passed I continued to indulge my passion. My father continued to take us to games, arriving early so we could see the visiting teams get off the bus, then patiently staying while we raced onto the turf at game's end to beg for chin straps and walk to the tunnel with our idols. My dad would always bring home a stack of newspapers on Monday so we could read or clip photos of the game. The *Examiner* used to have an entire page of "magic eye" photos taken by Matt Southard from the press box. They highlighted long runs and punt returns and had dotted lines and arrows. The *Chronicle* had green sports pages and the *Call-Bulletin* had pink. We thought both were pretty weird. Think of it, you're nine and they're laying green and pink sports pages on you...please! Like the *Examiner*, the *Call-Bulletin* had many photos. The *San Francisco News* and the *Oakland Tribune* had different photos and the *Los Angeles Times* always had big photos with the peristyle end of the Coliseum showing.

For Christmas in 1960 my parents got me a copy of Robert Reiger's book, *The Pros*. It was a watershed for me. For months I pored over the grainy black-and-white photos. They celebrated the players while heralding the game as the coming American spectacle — and it planted a subliminal seed in my head.

No longer was it enough to *be* at the games. I wanted to photograph them. I didn't know who to talk to in order to get on the field, but I noticed that the photographers usually wore coats and hats and had colored passes dangling from their coats. After a game in 1961, I found one on the field. I took it home, studied it, and decided to make one myself out of many different colors of paper. Next, I borrowed my dad's Ansco camera and, as a final touch, his London Fog coat. I was *almost* ready to rock and roll. I say almost because now I had to see if my passes worked. In those days security at Kezar consisted of about thirty uniformed San Francisco policemen ringing the track. I slipped over the rail and approached Officer Pope.

"Officer, I'm working on a book called *Sunday Gladiators* and no book on football would be complete without you guys. Would you mind grouping some of your colleagues around you?" They never even bothered me after that. Thus began my career in football photography.

When I went east to college in late 1964, I decided to call the PR men in both Washington and Baltimore to continue "working on my book." Those were different times and it was much easier for a young man with a little ambition and a lot of bullshit to ride a wave right down into the field.

From 1967 through 1972, I took a sabbatical from football and life. For me and many others of my generation, the late '60s was a heady time of experimentation, self-discovery, the global student revolution, and rock 'n' roll.

I began shooting the 49ers again in 1973. We were now playing in Candlestick Park — on plastic grass. It seemed so different from the '50s and '60s, but the game was as exciting as ever. I began to chronicle the 49ers in earnest. Before, I'd shot game action like everyone else, but on returning I had a different vision. I started shooting football the same way I shot bands. I shot as much with a wide-angle lens as long glass. I'd slip in front of players on the sidelines, crawl on my stomach, lie on my back shooting up. It looked insane but the angles and resulting pictures were just what I wanted. I remember showing a stack of sideline shots to someone at Associated Press in Los Angeles. "What's this shit? Let's see some action." I snatched the photos from his fist.

"Hey idiot, this is photojournalism. Don't you ever read *Rolling Stone*?" He hadn't.

I continued working mainly with black-and-white because I felt it was perfect, with the 24mm and 35mm lens, for capturing the intensity of the combatants along the sidelines. I was shooting the action that you couldn't see from the stands. It was the mood and intensity that for unknown reasons were rarely shown in books and

magazines. At NFL Properties in Los Angeles, Dave Boss encouraged me to delve more deeply into the action with my wide-angle. The more I shot on the sidelines, the more I felt there was even more to the game that people had yet to see and feel.

When I was shooting rock 'n' roll, the best moments were ones with the bands in the limos, backstage, before the show; musicians collapsing on a couch drenched in sweat with the roar of the crowd still in their ears. It was the same with football. I wanted my photos to take the consummate fan behind the scenes — to expose a world only the players and coaches were privileged to see. At this time everyone was switching to color, but this particular mood felt black and white...it *was* black and white. Can you imagine *On the Waterfront* or *The Hustler* in color?

The next frontier was the locker room. It was the parallel to backstage: a fantasy place where no fan had ever ventured. What was it really like at halftime? I wondered aloud to a number of photographers and football people. I was assured by one and all that it would be easier to gain access to the War Room in the Pentagon.

Well, maybe...but if you can hang out with Led Zeppelin and The Rolling Stones....

When I first approached Dave Boss with the idea he was very supportive. John Weisbusch, the editor of *Pro* and a good friend, was excited by the possibilities. They both

cautioned me that it wouldn't be easy, noting that only Herb Whiteman in St. Louis and Baron Wolman with the Oakland Raiders had gained locker-room access. I was buoyed by the fact that the 49ers had a new owner — Eddie DeBartolo, Jr., someone my age, and a new head coach, Bill Walsh. They both seemed *different* from the other owners and coaches around the league at the time. Dave and John decided to expand my idea into an assignment but left it to me to gain access. George Heddleston was the 49ers' Director of Publicity at the time, and I remember his pained looked when I first broached the idea, but he promised to speak with Coach Walsh about it. Coach was apprehensive and a bit skeptical at first, but he has a great sense of history and, I think, understood what I wanted to depict. He decided that as long as I could remain invisible and not deter either the players or the coaches from their pregame preparation or halftime adjustments I could operate on a "We'll-see-how-it-goes" basis. If I became too obtrusive with my camera, Coach Walsh had only to meet my eyes. Depending on the circumstance, I would back off or cease shooting altogether. During the first few weeks various players would ask what I was doing, but from then on players and coaches alike were, for the most part, unaware of the camera.

My intention with this book is to reveal a unique, unprecedented view of professional football in general and the San Francisco 49ers in particular. We begin in 1979 at the bottom of the mountain, with the team going 2-14, and we end in late January of 1989, in the locker room of Joe Robbie Stadium, Miami. You, the reader, are aboard for the entire 10-year trip. You ride the bus to the stadium, walk down the tunnel, feel the gut-convulsing tension of the pregame locker room, view the halftime adjustments, feel the pain, share the sideline blackboard strategy charts, revel in the postgame celebrations. In essence, you share everything but the actual pain and stiffness of a postgame Monday morning. I hope you find it as exciting and fulfilling as I have.

Like any project that spans 10 years, none of what has been depicted would have been possible without the inspiration and assistance of many people.

Photographers, both past and present, helped shape my vision. Chief among them were people like Matt Southard and the crusty veteran Bill Nichols of the *San Francisco Examiner*. Frank Ripon, the original 49ers archivist from their inception in 1946 through the mid-1980s. His photos of Albert, McElheney, Wilson, Nomellini, Tittle, Perry, et al., are legendary. Robert Reiger and his co-shooter Fred Roe chronicled the mid-to-late 1950s with their grainy, stark black-and-whites. Their photos remain to this day, some of the best ever. Vic Stein, for his panoramic views of Los Angeles Rams and LA Dons games in the Coliseum from the late 1940s through the mid-1960s. Vern Beiver, who captured the magic of the Lombardi Packers of the '60s. Herb Whiteman, who shot for the St. Louis Cardinals. He was the avatar of locker-room photojournalism. To my knowledge, he was the first...and the best. I still shake my

head in wonder when I look at his visions in the league's 1972 book, *The Pro Football Experience*. Walter Ioos, formerly on staff at *Sports Illustrated*, is probably the best at capturing the decisive moment of game action. His black-and-white photo of Ray Berry making a fingertip reception with toes inbounds against the 49ers in Baltimore is still one of my favorites — not to mention "The Catch" cover. Above and beyond this, Walter loved Elvis and still carries a picture of Little Richard in his appointment book. To paraphrase the King, "T.C.B. baby!"

Peter Read Miller, also of *Sports Illustrated*. He started with a grainy, punchy, cinema-verité black-and-white approach to present-day color freezes of the vital moment. Peter and I have discussed (argued) over the various approaches to shooting football — and living life — over the past 15 years. A better foil and devil's advocate I have yet to meet.

I could fill another chapter with the names of people who have helped me in this endeavor. Foremost among everyone would have to be "The Blues Brothers" at NFL Properties in Los Angeles. I'm talking about Dave Boss and John Weisbusch. Dave was there at the beginning and did as much as any single person to further my career in photography — both in and out of sports. John has suggested stories and assignments, and has generally egged me on both in football and in life. Sharon Kuthe has proven to be an invaluable player at the NFL Properties library. She has always come through and has a sense of humor, too.

Jim Heffernan, the Director of Public Relations for the NFL at league headquarters in New York has always been there to smooth out the rough spots and make the difficult easy. "Hef" combines a love of the game with an appreciation for characters. He is a rare individual indeed.

Steve Cassady, who wrote for the league, the Oakland Raiders, and John Madden in the '70s and early '80s. Not only a great *football* writer but a colorful product of the times, Steve made the men who played the game come alive.

You can't take pictures without cameras and lenses, and without the help over the years from my good friend at Nikon, Mike Phillips, I'd probably be shining shoes at the bus station today. Mike, and, on occasion, Ron Tanawakee in Los Angeles and Bill Pekela in New Jersey, have lent me cameras and lenses without which many of the images you see in this book wouldn't have been possible.

Without photo labs there would be no negatives, and in San Francisco, Tak Kuno at the Photo Lab has applied his particular brand of darkroom alchemy to my black-and-white negatives. At the New Lab, the wizards of color have consistently amazed me with their motivation and ability to do things no other color lab on the West Coast can do. Special thanks to Arsinio Lopez, Hugh Helm, and Touchdown Tommy Kunhardt, who babysit all the 49ers projects as if they were their own children. When the 49ers have needed color prints, Frank Bonfiglio at the Imperial Color Lab has performed masterfully. He remains a Sicilian craftsman without equal.

Special thanks to Dennis Desprois, my partner and friend in the early days with the team, and to James Perez and Bill Fox, excellent shooters in their own right who have lent their vision to assist the 49ers for the past few seasons. Butch Bridges and Keith Rendel have assisted me on the sidelines since 1981 and in that time they've pretty much done it all, from lugging cameras and lenses, to shooting and getting some of the shots I couldn't or didn't. And Kristin Sundbom, who has been with me since 1973. More than an assistant, she has done all of the above and more; her hand-tinting of locker room shots *made* the portfolio for the NFL league. Besides being an artist, my best friend, lover, and mother of our son Ari, Kristin has that special ability to refuse to allow my life ever to become boring. To Ari, thanks for being the best son anyone could ever want and for having the patience to allow me to work on this project before pitching your BP.

To Jay Schaefer, my editor, and Sharilyn Hovind at Chronicle Books for spending so many hours going through proof sheets, photos, caption sheets, and tall tales.

Thanks to an old friend, "Jungle" Jim Marshall, one of the great rock 'n' roll photographers, for his inspiration. And Baron Wolman. I was influenced by Baron from the very beginning. I mean how many of you remember he was the original *Rolling Stone* staff photographer, the editor of *Rags* magazine, the guy who brought you *The Roller Derby* and *California from the Air*? I'd always wanted to collaborate with Baron, and when he called me initially with his idea to produce a book on the Super Bowl years — to do all the what, where, when, why, and how — I jumped at the chance. Considering that he has allowed me to work on all the fun parts of this project, I look forward to working with him again.

Last, but certainly not least, I owe thanks to so many in the 49ers organization, and that includes everyone from the women in the office, to Bronco Hinek and Ted Walsh, to our trainers Lindsy McLean, Fred Tedeschi, and Ray Tuffs, who kept me healthy, to the coaching staff for putting up with me when I wasn't quite invisible. To George Heddleston, who helped me with the initial stages of this undertaking in the late '70s. To Keith Simon, who always has a sense of humor no matter how bizarre a story — or a request — can get. To John McVay for his understanding, patience, and graciousness. To the Yanagi family for their special way of viewing things. To Carmen Policy for always being helpful, always gregarious, and the perfect gentleman to have in your corner.

To the public relations staff: Dave Rahn and Cheryl Forbis, assistants in the publicity office, for their endless help and favors, and a very special thanks to Jerry Walker and Rodney Knox. More than just my bosses, they have been good friends and have doubled as troubleshooters, alter egos, father confessors, and stern taskmasters since 1981. Many of my projects would never have gotten beyond the drawing boards without their suggestions, advice, admonishments, and unending assistance. They've gone above and beyond the call of duty for me, and I could *never* thank them enough...even though there are times when they'd probably both agree that the only thing worse than having me for an enemy is having me for a friend.

To Coach Walsh. He has always been open and receptive to our ideas. Without his trust, his keen sense of history, and his willingness to try photographically what few have done before, many of the photos you see in this book would not have been possible. In his 10-year reign, the 49ers fortunes went from rags to riches. It has been a magic tenure. Thanks to the Coach, we all became the invisible 46th man — on the field, on the bench, in the locker room.

To Edward J. DeBartolo, Jr. — Mr. D to most everyone in the 49ers organization. When all has been said and done, he is the man who made most of this possible. When he took over as owner he transformed the San Francisco 49ers from an organization to a family — and a family in the truest sense of the word. He makes everyone in the organization feel they are valuable. He spares no expense, no emotion. He has given selflessly to each and all of us; no one here lacks the material means or the moral support to succeed. One can find many adjectives to characterize Mr. D — concerned, intense, passionate, volatile — but, more than anything else, he cares. His lust for life is evident in everything he does. Before him the 49ers were always colorful, sometimes exciting, but never reached that final reward. With his arrival we've been world champions three times to date.

To Mr. D, Coach Walsh, and all the 49ers players and fans past and present, thank you for such a fantastic journey.

Michael Zagaris

FOREWORD

Michael Zagaris, Team Photographer

Michael Zagaris has been there through all of the 49ers' magical seasons. He has been there with his camera recording the tense stillness before games, the marshaling of wills at halftimes, the ebbing of adrenalin in steamy postgame shower rooms. He has been there, on the inside, recording pro football history.

Zagaris's work is art, of course, but much of his art depends on proximity and timing. They are what makes these pages special, because for 10 years Zagaris has had what only a very few NFL photographers have had — complete family status with the 49ers.

An indelible image of Michael Zagaris appeared in January 1982, when CBS cameras invaded the tunnel in the Pontiac Silverdome moments before Super Bowl XVI, the first of the team's three championships in the decade. The cameras waited for the 49ers to surface from their pregame rituals, from their talks, their tapings, their meditations.

The tunnel was stark and poorly lit, a cylinder of rough concrete. When the wide double doors opened, the first man in camera range was Zagaris in his "game uniform" — a baseball hat and jersey, worn blue jeans rolled up at the ankles, and white football cleats. The camera stayed on him for an instant. His eyes were sunk into his head, his skin was chalk white. It was his game face — literally. The players clattered around him and he led them onto the field, leaping and gesturing.

Zagaris didn't just stumble into a close-range relationship with coach Bill Walsh and the 49ers players. He never was officially encouraged. He just sort of assimilated until he was as much a part of the inner circle as players, coaches, equipment men, and trainers. He did it with his talented eye, of course, but he also did it with his personality. The words "stop," "don't," "no," and "can't" are not in his vocabulary. It is an exaggeration to say he has had the status of player or coach. But he has seen all 10 years of the Walsh era from the same angle of vision.

Acceptance didn't come because he stayed silent in the background: he didn't. He simply proved he belonged. His constant rap with players endeared him, his feel and respect for football tensions and moods earned him acceptance.

From the way he started, it was almost inevitable that he would gain that kind of proximity.

Return to the civil turmoil of the late 1960s: Zagaris had just abandoned his ambition to become President of the United States. Seriously. He was an aspirant to Camelot, an impressionable teenager during the tragic short run of John F. Kennedy, and later a working member of both the Washington, DC, staff and presidential campaign of Robert F. Kennedy.

From a Wally-and-Beaver upbringing in different towns of northern California he had gone on to George Washington University in Washington, DC, played split end for the Fighting Colonials, and majored in Sino-Soviet Relations — so he could negotiate his own treaties when he became President, of course.

He had his future charted: he would try professional football with the team he idolized, the Baltimore Colts; return to California; attend law school; establish a practice; get elected to public office; and then scale his way up the political pyramid.

He was signed as a free agent by Buddy Young to the Colts' camp in the summer of 1967, but against competition from the likes of Lenny Moore, Ray Perkins, and Jimmy Orr, he lasted only a few days. Nobody had to ask for his playbook. He saw reality written on the wall and he left quietly of his own accord.

Weeks later he enrolled at the University of Santa Clara law school, ranking number two in his class after the fall semester. During the same season he washed out of the San Jose Apaches, a minor-league extension of the Oakland Raiders and, coincidentally, a team coached by one Bill Walsh.

The following spring, 1968, the map to Zagaris's future pointed in other directions. Martin Luther King was killed in April. Then Sirhan Sirhan downed his hero, Bobby Kennedy, two months later. It was too much for Zagaris. When he walked into his contract law final the next day the professor said, "I know you were close to the senator, I'm sorry." Then added, "But you'll have to take your final anyway."

A final it was. Zagaris filled in several blue books with a scathing extemporaneous essay on the ills of American society. After finishing, his pen still smoking, he took a bubble gum card from his pocket. The card had a transferable likeness of San Francisco Giants pitcher Juan Marichal on it. Zagaris took a coin from his pocket and rubbed the surface of the card, transferring the image to the blue book cover. Then he drew a dialogue balloon. In it he had Marichal saying, "Michael, thees ees all boolshit. Just peetch me a strike."

Thus ended his law career, his career in politics, his aspirations for the White House.

Zagaris drifted into a kind of counter-cultural self-reliance. He didn't exactly work, at least not on a career goal. He had jobs (from selling Fuller brushes to teaching junior high school in East Palo Alto), but his real pursuit was photography in the areas of his two real loves — rock music and sports.

As a prep school student in San Jose, he had snuck his way into 49ers games by forging sideline passes made from colored cardboard stock. He stood near benches during the Vince Lombardi era of professional football wearing a suit, a narrow tie, a wrinkled raincoat, and an

Ansco box camera hanging by a strap from his neck. At 15, he watched the games at close range, occasionally taking scrapbook snapshots of himself and his brother Bruce with George Halas or Jim Brown or Lenny Moore or Hugh McElheney. He was proud of his youthful enterprises.

The problem for the older Zagaris was still how to gain entry—but this didn't stop him for long. He merely invented assignments. Zagaris has great telephone skills. He fears conversation with no one. He passed himself off as a sports photographer on some mumbled speculative assignment for this magazine or that. He was granted regular access to training camp by the pre-Walsh 49ers and was given sideline passes for games. He used his invented assignments to learn his craft and build his portfolio. By the time it was good enough he was extremely marketable, at which point he was in business.

Then, as now, his work was truly his own. Though he shoots game action as well as anyone, it never has been his specialty. It's just something that puts him elbow-to-elbow with every other photographer on the sideline. What distinguishes his very best work is the way it ushers the viewer into the soul of professional football.

ABC-TV coined a phrase years ago—"up close and personal." Michael Zagaris's work is the epitome of that concept. He is happiest shooting with a short lens in black-and-white—the vision that this combination captures is revealed in the remarkably intimate photojournalism featured throughout this book.

"Most sports action photography is taken with what they call 'long glass,'" Zagaris says. "Telephoto lenses bring you closer to the action, even though as the photographer you're really not. I use wide-angle lenses, and to use wide-angle lenses you have to be right on top of your subjects, or right with them. It's more photojournalistic. It opens everything up. Pictures taken that way become more of a story, almost like a visual diary. It gives you the pictorial feeling that you're eavesdropping. That's why *Rolling Stone* magazine made such an impact initially.

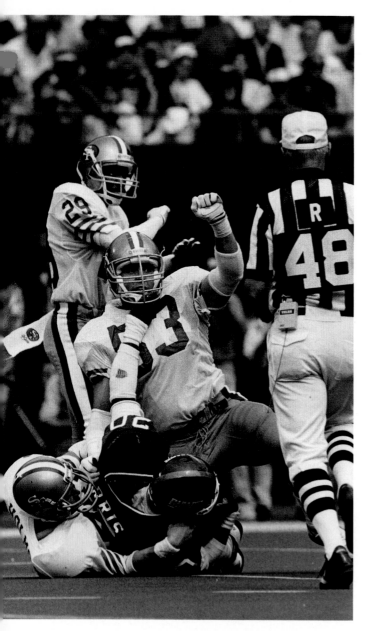

Moments later we invaded the CBS broadcast booth under the same guise. Soon Zagaris was taking pictures of Pat Summerall and Tom Brookshier as they scanned speed cards and exchanged pregame notes.

In the background at the time was a rookie announcer about to make a mark in his new profession, John Madden. Madden knew us from his days as head coach of the Oakland Raiders.

"What the hell are you guys doing here?" he asked, amused and sensing that maybe we shouldn't be there.

"Taking pictures," Zagaris said. "Smile, John."

Still, Zagaris takes what he does seriously. He never eats before games. He wants to be lean and hungry. He is in the locker room two hours before the game, plus at halftime and after the game. He materializes at the 50-yard line for coin flips. During the game, in full view and with approval of the players, he slips across the retaining chalk line into the bench area. He snaps short-glass images of players slumped on the bench sucking in oxygen through plastic masks, the scowl of a coach who has just seen a pass dropped, and the fiery eyes of a linebacker who has just come off the field after making a crushing hit.

On trips he never misses a Saturday practice, an event ignored by most media. On a Saturday in Buffalo in late December 1983, for instance, he captured a wonderful moment on the sidelines at Rich Stadium before the 49ers' workout. The players were wearing skin-diving gloves and watch caps. One of them scooped up snow from a bank near the wall, where the snowplows had pushed it. The player threw a clump. Soon a bunch of laughing players joined in, packing snow in their palms, hurling, and dodging.

Zagaris saw it and photographed it, the megasport of professional football brought to the level of kids engaged in a snowball fight on a winter Saturday afternoon.

In a game turning corporate too fast, a game that threatens to distance itself from its following because of a big business mentality, Michael Zagaris helps return the essence to the fans. His lens is our microscope. He proves that the game of football is still very human indeed.

Steve Cassady
Sportswriter and author of *Oakland Raiders: The Good Guys*

That's what Annie Leibowitz and Baron Wolman were doing with rock music. You're talking photojournalism."

Zagaris's approach is akin to vicarious gate-crashing. He and I collaborated often over the years, and I always watched his methods with fascination.

In January 1980, we found ourselves wandering through forbidden tunnels at the Rose Bowl hours before the kick-off of Super Bowl XIV. His assignment at the time was from the NFL itself, under the vague dictum of "recording the week."

We strolled by the officials' locker room. Zagaris had an idea. He knocked on the door and said he was on assignment from the league. A striped-shirt figure opened up, gave him a quizzical look, then gestured us in. All tension was thawed by Zagaris's endearing banter. Before long, he was snapping candid images of Super Bowl officials at rest before the biggest, most pressure-filled challenge of their year.

INTRODUCTION

The Sports Photographer

For a sports photographer, nothing can compare to the thrill of being on the sidelines of a professional football game. Like others fortunate enough to be involved with the sport, I can't imagine *not* being there on fall Sundays: the attraction is simply too powerful.

Stepping onto the sidelines of a football game for the first time is an overwhelming experience. It literally short-circuits your sense of reality for a few giddy moments, like an E-ticket ride at Disneyland. The stadium and the crowd seem to be an immense audible backdrop, fading into infinity. The playing field is a broad green plain that appears a lot larger from the sidelines than it does from up in the stands. The players also appear larger than life, with their protective padding and helmets. Yet one also realizes that there are men here who, even without the padding, have arms as large as most people's legs and legs as big as some people's chests.

But the thing that really fractures your sense of equilibrium while standing on the sidelines is the sight and sound of 22 men playing football right before your eyes. With the snap of the ball the ground trembles as some two-and-a-half tons of humanity attack one another with shocking fierceness. The sound of colliding bodies has a thunderous acoustical richness; the voices of men shouting and grunting with exertion contrast sharply with the staccato sounds of impact. And the swiftness with which some of the players cover the field is almost incomprehensible: a wide receiver can be 20 yards downfield in the blink of an eye. The whole experience is fascinating and disorienting...again and again and again.

Photographers are visual reporters, the people who record on film the onrushing history of this spectacular game. No matter how many words are written about football, it is impossible to comprehend fully the character of the game and the greatness of its players and coaches without the photographs.

Photographing a game requires intense concentration. I suspect I am not alone when I say I don't even notice the crowd. It's there, a sound backdrop. But it really is a nonentity. What is evident is the field, the players, and the game.

The experienced photographer knows the game and, most likely, the teams and their personnel. A photographer who has covered a team often enough will know their tendencies in given situations and will be able to anticipate where the next play will be directed. It is not uncommon to see a photographer move to another part of the field, guessing what will happen next. The good ones do it all the time.

To cover the game well a photographer must be prepared to submit to all kinds of abuse — withering heat, frostbite cold, monsoon rains, and blinding blizzards, or fields as mucky and smelly as swamps, artificial turf so hot that it burns through the soles of shoes, and fields so frozen that you can cut yourself on the icy turf.

The photographer has to be aware of himself and where he is at all times because it is possible to get hurt on the sidelines. In the heat of the game, players don't always let up just because a tackle is made and a whistle has blown. With large bodies accelerating at high speed, no play is over until it's really over — especially those that carry a group of players toward the sideline boundaries. Photographers have suffered broken bones and damaged equipment as a result of not being alert.

The enterprising photographer must be prepared to deal with any circumstance on the field, and most carry at least two cameras — the preferred telephoto and one that can be grabbed for shooting without focusing, usually mounted with a 50mm or 35mm lens. This lens is also useful for shooting in and around the bench. Looking through a 35mm wide-angle is like looking through the wrong end of a telescope; through a 600mm telephoto lens, the men appear larger than Macy's parade balloon figures. But each lens has its purpose, and photographers have their choice.

While the game is in progress the photographer must keep a checklist constantly in mind — the location of the ball on the field, the down, the time remaining, the 45-second clock, the two-minute warning, the substitutions, the injuries. Light meters must be checked and rechecked, especially on days when the weather changes frequently.

A successful game-action photographer has the eye-hand coordination of a fencing master. Out of a mob of 22 players he or she must be able to follow and focus as the subject moves up, down, and across the field, anticipating the action that will make the best shot, and then tripping the button that activates the shutter...all in a millisecond.

And even then, there's no way to be certain you got the shot you wanted until after the film is developed. Because the 35mm camera body that nearly everyone uses has a glass mirror that flutters when the shutter is tripped, the photographer doesn't actually see the moment that the film captures. An adage on the field is "If you saw it, you probably didn't get it."

When a photographer is "on," in full concentration and emotional involvement with the game, there's a wonderful feeling of being a part of the action. When a game is being decided in the final minutes, anticipating the sequence of plays becomes almost as heady as calling signals on the field. The interaction between photographer and football player becomes a symbiosis of action and reaction. The magic comes in capturing the reality of the game on single frames of film, in making an athlete's great effort available to be seen again and again.

Sports photographers are getting better and better, and one of the reasons is the sophistication of the equipment being manufactured by the top camera/optics makers. Today's photographer has a myriad of options and can choose from equipment that would have appeared only in a Buck Rogers comic strip in the 1930s and 1940s. As late as the 1950s, color film was virtually unheard of for sports-action photography. Not only was it costly and very slow, but also only very few publications featured color pages. Long telephoto lenses were rare: the 35mm was the standard bearer throughout most of the '50s. Motor drives were generally unknown. Even the photographers themselves looked different: in those days they would show up at the stadium wearing slacks, a white shirt and tie, and wing-tip shoes.

Despite the increased number and excellence of today's photographers, they remain coach-class citizens in the world of sports media, with first class reserved exclusively for sports writers. Writers sit in the press box, where the host team staff lavishes attention on them. Everything they can wish for is available, from hot pregame meals to predesignated seating to a steady flow of information on the game in progress. On the field below the photographers are left to their own devices, unaided by anyone. Their most important job is to find a secure — and dry — spot to store immensely valuable camera equipment. They are questioned by security guards, eyed suspiciously by players and coaches, yelled at by field officials, fed cold hotdogs and warm cokes at halftime, and usually sneered at by cheerleaders.

Of course, photographers do have their idiosyncrasies. They love to gossip and complain, and they live in mortal fear that someone else will get "the" picture from the game. They trade news on camera equipment and assignments as if every game day was some sort of convention. They eye each other's equipment nervously, afraid someone else will have the newest gadget. They speak a jargon that includes film speeds, meter readings, stadium light sources (tungsten or mercury vapor), shutter speeds, pushed film, and brand names.

Michael Zagaris of the San Francisco 49ers is one of this breed, yet in his own individual way, Zagaris stands apart from the breed. Maybe it's his absolute devotion to his work: no one expends more energy or uses more equipment. Or perhaps it's his open-faced approach to life, where there are no limits, only opportunities. Michael out-talks, out-hustles, out-shoots, and simply outdoes almost every other camera-toter in the business.

And his pictures work. They convey, with amazing conviction, a real sense of the people who play the game. In the pantheon of football photographers, Zagaris belongs to a group of superior artists who have helped document this huge, colorful sport in a way that will benefit fans of the game for years to come. Many of football's most golden, precious, painful, and glorious moments will be kept alive by the wonderful photographs of Michael Zagaris.

David Boss
Vice-President & Creative Director
NFL Properties

PROFILE Bill Walsh

Bill Walsh turned a 2-14 team into the team of the '80s, with three World Championships in eight years, and he did it with style. If the Raiders were the ruffians of the NFL, the 49ers were the gentlemen; fans could be proud of their team's demeanor as well as its success. There was no boasting, no taunting of opposing players. Walsh's 49ers have been a classy team, with a professionalism that mirrors their coach's attitude.

But it takes more than good manners to turn a team around so dramatically. How, in fact, did Walsh do it?

"I think I have a creative mind," Walsh says, "which I've been able to apply to football. And I've been willing to take a certain amount of risk. There have been mistakes, but we've done enough good things to make up for the mistakes."

COLMAR

Creativity. In one play-off game, Walsh used guard Guy McIntyre as a blocker in the backfield on goal-line plays; in another he used guard John Ayers to block blitzing linebacker Lawrence Taylor. In a strike game in '87, he went to the wishbone offense against the Giants, running the ball to set up a touchdown pass.

Creativity. "He has a mind which squares the circle — or just goes completely outside it," said admiring sports attorney Leigh Steinberg after observing Walsh working his wonders in the draft. Many coaches and personnel staff approach the draft straightforwardly, trying to get the best players they can with their picks. Walsh evaluates his needs and how he can best fill them. One year that meant trading up to get his great wide receiver, Jerry Rice. Another year, when the draft had many good players but few great ones, Walsh and his scouting staff traded down several times, ultimately winding up with 14 picks — and 8 players who were starters for the '88 championship team. Other times he has used his picks to trade for players like tight end Russ Francis and quarterback Steve Young, who were better players than he could have gotten in the draft.

Creativity. Walsh "scripted" 25 plays to start each game. "That actually started when I was an assistant to Paul Brown at Cincinnati," he says. "Paul wanted to know what we had to start the game, and I gave him 2 plays, then 4, later 6 or 8. At San Diego I got up to 15. When I was coaching Stanford, I started with 15, went to 20 and then 25.

"The advantage was that we could make use of everything we'd been working on in practice and that the players were comfortable with. And it was a lot easier to draw up those plays in a clinical atmosphere than to try to remember them during a game when all the noise and excitement sometimes makes it impossible to think clearly.

"With the 49ers, there have been games where we've gone through all 25 plays, click, click, click. In the worst case, we might have used only 5 or 10 of the 25. That happened when we would run up against a defense that just fooled us, and even then we tried to come back the next time to work something against it."

The scripting also kept 49er opponents off balance. In this age of the computer, coaches find it easy to draw up tendencies of other teams in specific down-and-distance situations. But because Walsh drew up his 25 plays without knowing what the situations would be, there was rarely any pattern to his playcalling.

But Walsh's creativity perhaps showed up most clearly in the approach he took to building his first champion team, in 1981. In the draft that year, the 49ers took three defensive backs: Ronnie Lott (University of Southern California), Eric Wright (Missouri), and Carlton Williamson (Pittsburgh). There was no gradual break-in for "the three"; Walsh started them all, along with free agent Dwight Hicks, from the first exhibition game.

"We made the decision to use all three because that way they would only be looking at each other. As far as they knew, the way they played was the way everybody in the NFL played. If they had been put in the position of having to beat out veteran players, the veterans would have held them back with the tricks and shortcuts they knew from playing in the league."

At the same time, Walsh made certain that Joe Montana would be the leader the team needed by trading his first quarterback, Steve DeBerg. In Montana's first year, Walsh had built up Joe's confidence by using him in situations where he would look good, such as inside the other team's 20. In his second year, Joe took over as the starter in mid-season.

"But I knew that as long as Steve was around Joe would never be able to assert himself," says Walsh. "Steve is a quiet person and a very pleasant, likeable guy. But underneath that, he's a tenacious competitor. The team needed to identify one strong leader, and Joe was the player."

So Walsh traded DeBerg, leaving Montana in control. The rest is history.

Even Walsh was surprised at the state of the 49ers when he took over as head coach and general manager in 1979. "I knew there wasn't much talent, but I thought, with our system, that we'd be able to win five or six games," he says. "But I'd made some serious miscalculations.

"I thought we'd at least have a solid front four on defense. I'd been told that. But I found out that Jimmy Webb was nearing the end of his career, and so was Cleveland Elam. Cedrick Hardman could still play, but his personality wasn't good for the team. He'd been in a position where he was on a team with a lot of veterans, so he could wisecrack and basically be an individual. Now he was all alone in a sense because his older teammates were gone, and he couldn't help us. So what I thought was a strength was a weakness.

"And I had thought that O.J. Simpson still had something left. I thought when his knee got better he'd be able to help us. But I learned that O.J. had an arthritic knee which hurt him all the time. He didn't want to do anything on it because of the pain, let alone play."

But if that first year — the second straight 2-14 season for the 49ers — was painful, the second year was worse.

"The first year we moved the ball and scored some points, and our fans came to the games thinking we had a chance. But that second year we won our first three games and then lost eight in a row. That was the worst, because I wondered if we'd ever win another game.

"In that third game that we won, we lost running back Paul Hofer, who was our one big offensive talent at the time. People underestimated Paul. They talked about his heart, his courage — and he certainly had that. But he was a better player than they realized. He had the knack of making tacklers miss by just that much."

The 49ers righted themselves, winning three of the last five and almost winning another, against Buffalo. One of their three wins still ranks as the top comeback in NFL history. Trailing 35-7 at halftime, they beat New Orleans in overtime, 38-35.

The next year the 49ers bolstered their defense with three defensive backs, by signing free agent linebacker Jack Reynolds, and trading for pass rushing defensive end Fred Dean. Meanwhile Montana and Dwight Clark turned into an exciting and effective pass-and-catch duo.

That team, the first 49er Super Bowl champion, had almost no running: Ricky Patton led the team with 543 yards. So Walsh devised an offense in which he used short passes — almost long handoffs — to control the ball in the way that other coaches used running plays.

That became known as the "Walsh offense," but it was only the first example of what Walsh regards as another important reason for his success: the ability to make the maximum use of his personnel.

In future years he would modify his offense to make use of Jerry Rice's ability to catch long touchdown passes. When he had two effective running backs, Wendell Tyler and Roger Craig, he used Tyler as the main running threat and used Craig as both a runner and pass catcher; as a result, Craig became the first back in NFL history to gain 1000 yards in both running and receiving in the same year.

Finally, in the 1988 season, he modified his offense again so that Craig was second in the conference in rushing, with 1,502 yards.

Opposing coaches realized, to their dismay, that the one constant in the Walsh system was winning.

The Walsh teams were always known for their ability to keep other teams off balance. Part of that was mental, because of the unpredictability of the Walsh system, but a big part was also physical. Walsh coached his players to hit hard and to hit fast.

"We've always told the players they should hit the other players a split-second before they get hit," he says. "If you're on defense, hit that blocker before he gets set. If you're on offense, block the defensive man before he makes his move.

"I've likened it to a championship fight, where the champion lands his jab just a split second before the challenger lands his, so even though it looks like an even fight, the challenger is taking much more punishment. In the final rounds, he's beat down.

"It's the same way in a football game. If you get on top of your opponent early, you're going to have the advantage late in the game. The closest example would be the Cleveland Browns of the '50s, who always seemed to be just a little bit ahead of everybody."

Technical football by itself, though, doesn't win games. Walsh believes the personal side was just as important in his success. "I take a certain approach when dealing with people," he says, "and a big part of that approach is humor."

The most famous incident in the Walsh years came when the team arrived in Detroit for its first Super Bowl and Walsh greeted them at the hotel in a bellman's uniform. But more important has been the day-to-day atmosphere around the team. "It's not that we have a lot of bathroom humor type jokes on the practice field," he says, "but we've enjoyed it out there."

That kind of atmosphere, in turn, has fostered one in which players have taken on responsibility. "A coach can only do so much," says Walsh. "What you need — and what we've had on the 49ers — has been players taking it on themselves to tell other players what needs to be done.

"We've constantly stressed responsibility. When a receiver catches a pass, we make sure he understands that he's catching it only because the blockers have blocked for him and the quarterback has thrown the pass. He's not just catching the ball for himself; he's catching it for 10 other people. It's the same way for a defensive back stopping a pass; he's doing it for his 10 teammates on the field."

For Walsh, there was no better example of the character of his teams than in the '88 season.

"We had lost to Phoenix in the closing seconds," he remembers. "The next week we lost to the Raiders in what was probably the low point of my career here.

"At that point we were 6-5. Many thought we would pack it in, maybe win 2 or 3 more games the rest of the way, and finish 8-8, or even 7-9.

"But this team, instead of falling apart, pulled together. I've never seen a team closer than we were that week. We beat the Redskins that week in what was the key to the season and went on to win four out of our last five.

"Then we went on to play two nearly perfect games in the play-offs. Our game in Minnesota was the best game we'd played in years. Our Super Bowl win over Miami (January 1985) had been like that, an almost perfect game. And then our game against the Bears in Chicago was as good as the Minnesota game. Those are the kinds of games coaches love, because you can play the games back on tape and just enjoy them."

The Minnesota win was especially satisfying because the loss to the Vikings in the play-offs the previous January had been the most galling of his career. "We were the best team in the league," he says. "We'd probably made too much of the Rams game (which the 49ers won, 48-0). They'd lost (quarterback) Jim Everett, so they were without their star and leader. It was hard to get some of the players going again after that game, and we weren't as well prepared for Minnesota as we should have been.

"This time it was just the opposite. We'd lost to the Rams, and that was a motivating factor. Minnesota came in thinking that they'd almost beat us in the regular season and they wouldn't be beat again by a play like Steve Young's run. But we just stayed on top of them all the way."

That made 1988 perhaps the most satisfying of Walsh's 10 with the 49ers, but the demons that drove him to

success also drove him from the sidelines.

Walsh has always seemed almost professorial on the sidelines, the clipboard adding to the dignified air. He always seemed in total control. But inside he's been a volcano, stomach churning, nerves screaming.

"I'm too sensitive," he admits. "I react to criticism when perhaps I shouldn't. Writers say I'm callous when I get rid of older players, but it's just the opposite. I agonize over it. I agonize over the losses too much, I know."

That difference between the public perception and the private reality is not surprising; for a man who has been in the public eye for so long, Walsh has managed to keep his personality and thoughts private to a remarkable degree.

To those few people he trusts and respects Walsh can be warm and witty, often poking fun at himself. A model of organization on the field, he admits to being totally disorganized away from it. "I can never find the pink slip for my car," he says.

There is one public perception of Walsh that is dead-on accurate, though: he is a perfectionist. He once said that after every game — even the Super Bowl win over Miami — he has gone back over his playcalling and picked out plays he would like to have changed. Though he was happy to go out a winner with the Super Bowl win over Cincinnati, he was extremely frustrated by the game.

"I haven't even looked at the films of that game," he admits. "It wasn't a classic win. Our defense played very well for the whole game, but we just couldn't get untracked offensively until the fourth quarter."

In Walsh's mind there's a picture of the perfect season and the perfect career. The near misses, like '83, when the 49ers fell just two controversial penalties short of beating the Washington Redskins in the NFC championship game, haunt him. "I don't know if we were the best team in the league that year," he says, "but I think a 49ers-Raiders Super Bowl would have been very exciting."

In his mind there is even an asterisk after the '84 season, with the team he regards as his best. "We could easily have been undefeated that year," he says. "We lost to Pittsburgh on a questionable pass-interference call."

To those of us who look at his record objectively, not measuring it against an unattainable standard of perfection, it's obvious that Walsh ranks with the greatest coaches of all time, especially considering the conditions under which he has operated.

Some of the coaching legends of the past, like George Allen, Vince Lombardi, and Paul Brown, won at a time when the NFL had no more than 12 teams; Walsh had to beat out 27 teams. Chuck Noll won four Super Bowls with Pittsburgh, the only coach to top Walsh's three, but he won them with a team which was basically intact for the whole stretch; Walsh won three Super Bowls with three different teams, with only Montana, Randy Cross, and Ronnie Lott as key players on each team. Some successful coaches, like John Madden and Tom Landry, coached the team while others in the organization got the players; Walsh did both.

Best of all, he did it in San Francisco. Thanks for the memories, Bill.

Edward J. DeBartolo, Jr.

It's impossible to overestimate the importance of owner Edward DeBartolo, Jr., to the 49ers' success in the '80s. At a time when meddling owners are the rule rather than the exception in the NFL, DeBartolo has let Bill Walsh, the coaches, and the front office staff do their jobs without interference, and the results have been gratifying.

"Once Bill got here, I stepped back from it," says DeBartolo, reminiscing about the dozen years he's owned the club. "With the corporation work I have in Youngstown, it was just too much for me to get involved with the club. And it didn't make any sense for me to be making decisions on football matters.

"There are times when I get involved on monetary matters now, but I don't want to have to be in the situation of making a decision on players. That's for football people. That's why Bill was the executive vice president for football operations. He was making the decisions, and he did a good job."

Possibly even more important, DeBartolo has never pinched pennies with the 49ers. The club has had very few salary disputes with players because DeBartolo has put winning ahead of the bottom line.

Some clubs haggle with top draft choices and don't sign them until well into training camp or even into the season, so the players are of no value during their first season. But under DeBartolo the 49ers almost always sign their draft picks before the start of camp, and many — including Ronnie Lott and Jerry Rice — have been big factors in their rookie years.

Walsh has had virtual carte blanche, too, when he's gone after other players.

The first example came in 1981, when Fred Dean, an extraordinary pass rusher, was locked in a salary dispute with the San Diego Chargers. Dean had signed a long-term contract earlier in his career and wanted to renegotiate. The Chargers refused and traded him to the 49ers, who gave Dean the contract he wanted.

Walsh had long felt that a strong pass rush was one of the most important factors in a team's success and Dean soon proved that, becoming such a force that fans soon started chanting, "Dean-fense." Without question, the 49ers would not have been a Super Bowl team in '81 without Fred Dean.

Six years later DeBartolo showed his willingness to open his pocketbook again when the 49ers traded for Tampa Bay quarterback Steve Young; as a condition of the deal, DeBartolo agreed to repay Tampa Bay for Young's $1 million signing bonus.

With the Young trade the 49ers were essentially paying for two first-string quarterbacks, and Joe Montana's salary was already more than $1 million yearly. "I don't know any other clubs that would have been willing to do that," said Walsh after the trade, "but Eddie knew how important it was for us to make the deal."

When Montana was injured late in the '87 season, Young quarterbacked the team to wins over Chicago, Atlanta, and Los Angeles. When Montana was sidelined again midway through the '88 season, Young beat the tough Minnesota Vikings with a remarkable 49-yard touchdown run in the final minutes of the game.

"It's hard to make money with sports franchises if you really have that burning desire to win," says DeBartolo, explaining his theory of ownership. "Even with the TV contract we have, this isn't a big money-making business. We made a couple of bucks, and I do mean a couple, this past year, but we're never going to make a lot of money out of the 49ers. I'd be happy if we just broke even or made a couple of bucks every year. Winning is the most important thing.

"I know there are other clubs that feel different about this, and I'm not criticizing them. They do what they have to do, and we do what we have to do. It just doesn't seem to me that this is something you go into to make money."

DeBartolo notes wryly that other clubs now seem to be following the 49ers' lead. "When I look around," he says, "I see other clubs passing us up in spending. Some of the things that went on with the free agent thing [when the NFL created a program allowing some movement of players, after clubs had protected 37 players] are just unbelievable to me."

The San Francisco 49ers have had only two owners in their 43-year history: the Morabito family (and friends) and the DeBartolo family, which bought the club in 1977. It was a natural move for the DeBartolo family, which has been very involved in sports, from horse racing to hockey; the family, in fact, also owned a franchise in the USFL in the '80s.

"We first got a call from Joe Thomas, who'd been a lifelong friend — he was born in Cortland, Ohio, just about 10 miles north of Youngstown — that the 49ers franchise was available," remembers DeBartolo. "He'd gotten his information from Al Davis, who got a finder's fee in the deal. I think it was the only NFL franchise that was available at the time.

"There were numerous negotiations after that, but we closed the deal in time for me to go to the March meeting of NFL owners in 1977. I was involved more that first two years than I am now, but I didn't know anything about football. Not that I know a lot now, but I know more than I did then."

Thomas came with the deal, of course. It seemed to make sense because Thomas, though an opinionated man who often alienated those he worked with, had been a successful builder of teams at Miami and Baltimore.

From the start, though, the Thomas move was a disaster. Popular coach Monte Clark, who had nearly made the play-offs with the 49ers the year before, resigned because he felt he couldn't work with Thomas. Determined to make the 49ers his own, Thomas dismantled the team and made some fatal mistakes, including releasing Jim Plunkett, who went on to quarterback the Raiders to a Super Bowl championship in 1980, and trading a number one draft pick for a washed-up O.J. Simpson. The 49ers went through three coaches in two years — Ken Meyer, Pete McCulley, and Fred O'Connor.

To his credit, DeBartolo recognized that Thomas was a mistake and fired him after the 1978 season. At first he thought of looking for both a general manager and coach, but soon he realized that one man could fill both jobs — Bill Walsh, who had had two successful years as head coach at Stanford.

"Hiring Bill Walsh was something that happened very fast," DeBartolo says. "I had followed his career at Stanford somewhat, and after the Bluebonnet Bowl [won by Stanford] I called him to set up a meeting. We met at the Fairmont Hotel the next week.

"You know how you can meet a person and know right away that he's going to do great things? That's the way it was when I met with Bill. He was such a forceful, intelligent man. We only met for about 40 minutes and we did a lot of sparring back and forth, but I think we both knew in that time that he was going to be the coach.

"We had talked to other guys about being general manager, but after talking to Bill, I just felt he had administrative ability as well as coaching ability, so I gave him the authority to handle all the football end of it. We had John McVay and John Ralston, who were doing most of the administrative work.

"There were some rocky times the first two years Bill coached the team, but you could see that he was headed in the right direction. He's done a great job. He's done everything that I could ever have hoped he would do."

Probably nobody has enjoyed the 49ers' success more, and deservedly so, than Eddie D., whose family took out a full-page ad in *USA Today* on his 40th birthday, calling him "The No. 1 49er."

"The 49ers have been the biggest and best thing in my life outside my family, of course," he says. "It's been a great experience for me. I've gotten to know the West Coast, to a point where I could see eventually making my home there — although not to run the 49ers. I wouldn't wish that on anybody.

"These last 10 years have been great ones. There's been a lot of emotion, not always positive, but a lot of fun. I wouldn't have traded this experience for anything."

Pregame

RIGHT: *August 4, 1987; Rocklin. In what has become an annual ritual, 49er players engage in a fishing derby competition in a stocked pool at camp.* BELOW: *September 3, 1986. Co-pilot Russ Francis points the way to Tampa. Each player has empty seats to his front and right to enable him to stretch out and relax.* FAR RIGHT: *January 17, 1982. Bill Walsh, disguised as a bellman, greets the team arriving at the hotel in Pontiac, Michigan, for Super Bowl XVI.* PREVIOUS PAGE, LEFT: *September 14, 1986; Anaheim Stadium. In the tunnel between the locker room and the field in Anaheim.* PREVIOUS PAGE, RIGHT: *July 1979; Santa Clara. New head coach Bill Walsh greets the 49ers at summer camp in Santa Clara. Beginning the last week of preseason and throughout the season the team practices at Santa Clara.*

July 1987; Rocklin. In the sweltering heat of mid-afternoon the 49er offensive line tackles the seven-man sled. More than half the players who arrive at camp do not make the team.

LEFT: *January 6, 1985; Candlestick Park. Head trainer Bronco Hinek applies compressed air to the helmet of Randy Cross prior to the championship game against the Bears. The air fills a compartment in the helmet and adjusts the fit, acting as a shock absorber.*

BELOW: *November 25, 1984; Superdome, New Orleans. Late in the season, Roger Craig adjusts voltage of his acupuncture needles before the game. Several players use acupuncture to facilitate quicker healing of their injuries.*

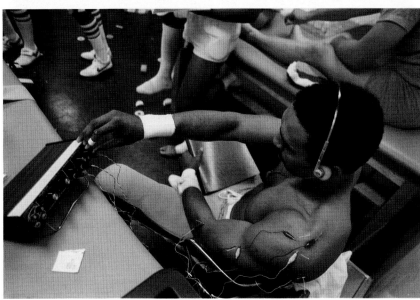

ABOVE: *October 27, 1985; Anaheim Stadium. Best friends Dwight Clark and Joe Montana share a moment before taking the field against the Rams.* LEFT: *November 16, 1980. Ray Wersching waits to take the field before a humid night in Miami. Wersching, the team's all-time leading scorer, played eleven seasons for the 49ers before retiring at age 39 in September 1988.* FAR LEFT: *November 11, 1985; Mile High Stadium, Denver. Head trainer Lindsy McLean tapes the knee of Bubba Paris.*

ABOVE: *July 30, 1988; Crystal Palace, London. Ronnie Lott, Joe Montana, director of public relations Jerry Walker, and Jerry Rice scan the London tabloids.*
RIGHT: *September 23, 1984; Veterans Stadium, Philadelphia. Joe Montana tries on special pads to protect his injured ribs prior to a game with the Eagles.*

ABOVE: *October 26, 1986; County Stadium, Milwaukee. Guards Randy Cross and John Ayers in the ten minutes between warm-up and the game.* RIGHT: *September 14, 1980; Candlestick Park. Hal Wyatt adjusts speakerphone on the back of Steve DeBerg as Sam Wyche goes over plays. Quarterback DeBerg was suffering laryngitis—hence the innovative speaker to amplify his voice during the game.*

LEFT: *January 22, 1989; Miami, Florida. 49er offense in different moods of contemplation prior to taking the field before the kick-off of Super Bowl XXIII. Left to right: Steve Young, Tom Rathman, Roger Craig, Jerry Rice.* BELOW: *September 11, 1988; Meadowlands, New York. Charles Haley taping his shoulder pads. Haley, like most 49er lineman, tapes the pads prior to each game to keep them smooth and difficult for offensive linemen to hold.*

RIGHT: *August 20, 1988; San Diego.*
Youthful 49er linemen looking
contemplative before a preseason
kick-off. Left to right: Jeff Bregel, Larry
Clarkson (who did not make the team),
Steve Wallace, and veteran Bubba
Paris. BELOW: *September 23, 1984;*
Veterans Stadium, Philadelphia.
Bubba Paris deep in concentration, his
knees scarred by many football wars.
FAR RIGHT: *November 11, 1985; Mile*
High Stadium, Denver. Ronnie Lott
prepares for cold weather as Gandor
looks on.

RIGHT: *September 2, 1984; Silverdome, Pontiac, Michigan. Dwaine Board and Larry Pillers stretch themselves in the spacious Silverdome locker room.*
BELOW: *September 8, 1983; Minneapolis, Minnesota. Ron Ferrari and Bill Ring stretch each other out in the locker room before taking the field. Every player has his own rituals for loosening up.*

LEFT: *September 9, 1987; Riverfront Stadium, Cincinnati. Offensive linemen in various stages of pregame preparation. Left to right: Bruce Collie, Guy McIntyre, Jesse Sapolu, Fred Quillan, Randy Cross, and Keith Fahnhorst.* BELOW: *October 18, 1987; Candlestick Park. Dwaine "Pee Wee" Board chats with Doctor Harry Edwards, a sociologist at the University of California, who has been with the team since 1985.*

ABOVE: *January 20, 1985; Super Bowl XIX; Stanford. Coach Bill Walsh, resting with quiet confidence moments before the team takes the field to defeat Miami.*
LEFT: *January 20, 1985; Super Bowl XIX; Stanford. Forty Niner players kneel during pregame prayer in the showers.*

Joe Montana

Joe Montana is best known for his incredible ability to make winning plays when the game is on the line. Among many, the most famous are the drive and touchdown pass that beat Dallas in the NFC championship game following the 1981 season and the winning touchdown drive and pass in the closing minutes of the 1989 Super Bowl.

In college Montana had the same reputation: he brought Notre Dame back from a 34-13 fourth-quarter deficit to beat Houston on the last play of the game in the Cotton Bowl. Despite that, he lasted until the third round of the NFL draft before being picked by the 49ers. He moved into the starting lineup midway through his second year and has been among the NFL's elite ever since.

As courageous as he is talented, Montana came back after back surgery in 1986, missing only seven games. His back troubled him again in the '88 season, but he returned

to lead the 49ers to four wins in their last five games and a triumphant return to the Super Bowl.

Joe also developed a close friendship with Dwight Clark, which is still a big part of his life though Clark has retired.

■ My friendship with Dwight has been special. We became roommates as rookies and we stayed roommates and became friends. Friends and competitors. We used to play the video games for hours. He was competitive and so was I, and we had fun at it.

I think a lot of our friendship was that we were both on the same side of the line of scrimmage. We sort of needed each other, not only for friendship but because he was away from South Carolina and I was away from South Bend and Pennsylvania. It gave us something to bring us a little closer together because we could practice together and share our college thoughts.

We were coming to a team that had lost 14 games. We knew we'd have an opportunity, but we also knew we'd have a growing stage. Fortunately, the growing stage was pretty short. I never envisioned that it would happen this quickly.

You have those dreams and you hope, but you never really believe they're happening. You pinch yourself to make sure it's happening.

When Dwight retired and the 49ers had a ceremony for him at halftime — well, in a way it was a great feeling to see him out there, seeing how much people appreciated having him play for the 49ers. But it was like a part of the 49ers was leaving, especially for me, as much as he'd contributed and sacrificed and worked for that team. It was sad to see him go.

Dwight will always be remembered for the touchdown catch he made that won the NFC championship game against Dallas [in 1982]. I'm often asked to compare that drive and the one that won the Super Bowl in '89. Both drives will be remembered in different ways. The one against Dallas will be remembered because it got us into our first Super Bowl. It was a dramatic thing, and Dwight made a great catch.

And it was done a little differently because there were a lot of running plays, though it ended with a pass. They were expecting us to throw because we'd done so much passing during the season.

The play selection in Miami [Super Bowl XXIII] was different because we not only won the game with a pass but we threw the ball all the way down the field. We were in

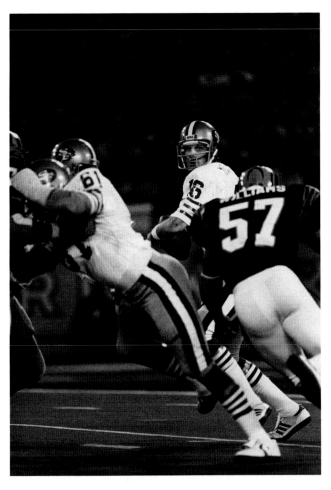

the two-minute offense, hurry up, calling some of the plays from the line of scrimmage. So they were completely different drives in that sense.

I don't think we audibled that much in the Dallas game. We had more time than we had in Miami. Against Cincinnati we called the plays from the line of scrimmage because we had to. I think there were four or five plays like that during the drive.

At times like that you get into a certain mode on the field and everything else is blocked out, like how much time is left. It's really secondary at that point. You're really trying to live each play for that play and not looking forward to the next play because if you don't keep the ball moving, you won't have anything. I guess you can call it living for the moment.

The last drive was different because I hyperventilated. It was crazy. It had never happened to me before. I guess it was the excitement, maybe a little bit of the weather. At that point you couldn't hear, so I was yelling plays at the top of my voice. Maybe it was because I used all of my oxygen — I had to call everything about eight times — and it took everything I had. I was just standing there and I went blank. I thought I was going to completely pass out.

When I walked up to the center I thought for sure I was going to call time-out. When I got up there it felt like it took minutes, but watching the film it went by just like that. In fact, it looked like I didn't even hesitate. But on the film I could see myself kind of swirling and I could remember the feeling — if you've held your breath too long or stood up too quickly, that's what it felt like.

And then I thought it would go away and it started to clear a little bit, so I got under the center and gave the snap count. But as I took my first step the movement brought it all back again, so I just stepped back and threw it in Jerry's direction....

The Super Bowl games were all different. Winning the first Super Bowl was great but the game wasn't that great, I didn't think, by either team. So it was a little disappointing in that sense, but it was still great to win it.

The next Super Bowl was the kind of game you like to be involved in, as an offensive or defensive player, because everything went the right way for us. So that's a great memory because we had such a great day offensively.

The last one was sort of a combination of the two, a little bit sweeter in one respect: last season they kind of counted us out halfway through the year, but then we came back. The Super Bowl wasn't that good of a game, but offensively it turned out to be a little better when we got going in the second half. Defensively we played well the whole game. It was a dramatic ending to a crazy year.

Playing for Bill Walsh, I think the biggest thing is that he helped me in understanding that you don't always have to throw the ball way downfield, like people want. You have to keep the pressure on. Sometimes if you throw Roger [Craig] the ball in the flat he's going to make just as many yards as if you throw the ball to a guy 10, 12, 15 yards down the field and he gets tackled immediately.

Bill was always very positive and instilled that in his quarterbacks: you always need to get something out of a play; if you do get sacked, you don't need to get it back right away. We had everything worked out with his offense. I thought it was a great system for a quarterback to be in because you always have some place to go with the ball. You don't have to take the big risk in going downfield unless the opening is there. It allows you to keep the ball moving. It also helps everybody's confidence because it allows you to spread the ball around.

You know it's funny, but games don't stick out for me. Some of the guys can tell you what plays happened, remember this drive, remember that one. It's like the way I remember the offense — you play that game, you go on to the next one. It's hard to think about the game when I'm still involved in it. I know we've accomplished a lot, and maybe when it's over I'll think about it. But I feel I'm not to the end of the book yet.

Ronnie Lott

Ronnie Lott has been a defensive star from the moment he arrived in 1981. His dedication and fierce, all-out style of play have inspired his teammates — just as they inspired his teammates at USC, where he was named Most Valuable Player and Most Inspirational in his senior year.

Ronnie started his 49er career at cornerback and moved to free safety in the 1985 season. He has been All-Pro at both positions.

With 43 career interceptions, he trails only Jimmy Johnson (47) in the 49ers' history. As a rookie he had seven interceptions and set a club record by returning three for touchdowns, only the second rookie in NFL history to accomplish that. In 1986, despite a hairline fracture in the shinbone of his right leg, he tied a team record with 10 interceptions, returned for 134 yards.

As mild-mannered off the field as he is ferocious on it, Lott has been involved in several charitable events in the South Bay, where he plans to continue to live after retirement, and he is a co-investor with past and present teammates in the Sports City Cafe in Cupertino.

■ When I was drafted by the 49ers my first thought was: "Now I can stay in California." I knew they needed defensive backs bad, real bad, so I wasn't surprised when they put me in the starting lineup right away. I was a little surprised when they put me at cornerback. There had been a lot of talk that I'd be playing safety in the pros.

It was funny about that season because we didn't really have any goals. We just wanted to play hard. I think the game that made the difference in our season was the third game, against Atlanta. We got our butts whipped [34-17] and we got pushed around pretty good. We just decided that we'd do the same thing they were doing, just play hard and beat up on people.

Cornerback was a challenge to me because a lot of people thought I couldn't play it. Playing safety is much different; the challenge there is that people expected I'd play it well, so I had to prove that I could do it.

I was reluctant to move to safety, partly because Dwight Hicks [who moved from safety to corner] was my friend, but mostly because we'd accomplished so much as a secondary, and I knew that would be over when we made changes.

Playing safety allows me to use more of my athletic skills, so in that sense it's a more satisfying position for me. I call defensive signals, too, and that's been a real learning experience. One mistake calling signals and a lot of people are going to be upset with you because they'll look bad.

I always felt I was a leader from Day One with the 49ers, but everybody talked about Dwight being the leader of the secondary so I let it go at that. I think one of the good things about our secondary is that everybody has developed as a leader in his own way.

I know some people think that if I didn't play so hard I wouldn't get hurt as much, but I can't see myself letting up at all. I look at it this way: there are a lot of people in regular jobs who have to go all-out, even when things aren't perfect for them, so I don't see how I can let up. That's always been my style of play, even as a kid. I don't know any other way to play.

I'm yelling at my teammates all the time. I don't believe some of the words that come out of my mouth at times; I use all the four-letter words. I'm like a wild man out there on the field. But I've always been that way. I was pretty feisty even as a rookie. I remember Hacksaw Reynolds telling me I had to learn to control my temper. That's really something, a guy like Hacksaw telling me that; he had a

pretty good temper himself. But the one thing I have learned over the years is which guys to yell at and which guys to leave alone.

Off the field it's been a different matter. I call myself the "fellowship director" because I get along with everybody. There's never been just one guy I've hung out with. I've always felt I was friends with everybody on the team.

To me, the most memorable game of my years with the 49ers was the regular season game against Dallas in 1981. That was really something because of all the hoopla surrounding the game, all the things that had transpired between the 49ers and the Cowboys over the years, and what the Cowboys represented as a football team. I remember when even our own fans were saying, "You can't beat the Cowboys." And then we beat them, real bad [45-14]. And it was especially big to me because the guy who really taught me how to play football, Dennis Thurman, was playing for the Cowboys.

Of course that first year, '81, was memorable because the first championship is always the one that sticks in your mind. What I remember most about that year, though, is how much fun we had. Everybody on that team just kind of hung together. That's the greatest thing in life, when you can have fun and win, too.

But a close second, maybe even a tie, was 1986. We had so many injuries and problems that year. Joe Montana was out with back surgery. But we still got into the playoffs. For me personally it was my most satisfying year. To have a broken bone and to come back and have my best year statistically, well, that made me feel pretty good.

What I remember most about the first Super Bowl was that Eric Wright made an interception which sealed the win for us. I thought that was fitting because I remembered that Eric had kinda got us started with an interception in the last exhibition game against Seattle that set up our win. So he got us started and he closed off the season.

To tell you the truth, the actual game wasn't that memorable. For one thing, I just knew we were going to win, so it wasn't a big surprise to me. And after playing for two years before 100,000 people in the Rose Bowl, it was no big deal to be playing before 60,000 people — in all that cold weather, too.

But the '84 game really was something special. To win in front of your home fans — that was really a big thrill. We'd set our goals at the start of the year and we'd accomplished everything we'd set out to do. And to shut out the "Mark Brothers" [Mark Duper and Mark Clayton] was special, too. All week we'd been reading that no cornerbacks could cover Duper and Clayton, so it was a special feeling to be able to shut them down.

It's been a great time, and when you're looking for reasons for our success, you have to start with Bill Walsh. When teams do well it always starts with the people at the top.

With us it's Bill and Eddie DeBartolo. There's been friction at times, but that's the price you pay when you've got people who want to win. Things can't be hunky-dory all the time. I'm sure there have been times when I haven't agreed with Bill on the way he's done things, but the bottom line is, we've won.

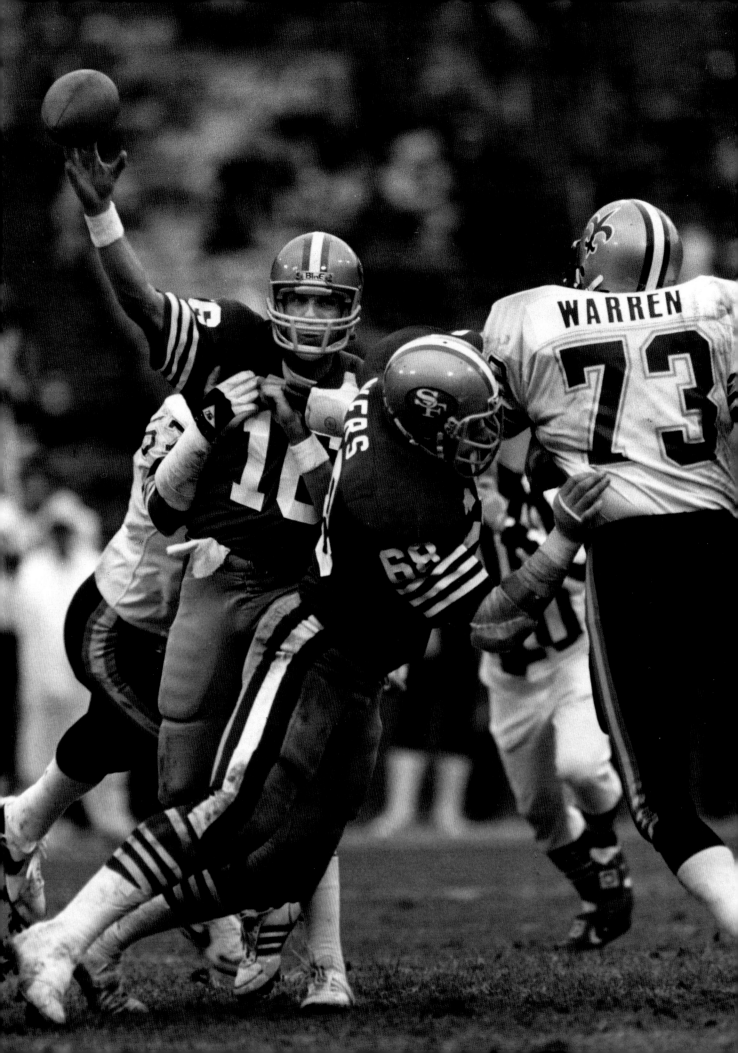

1st Half

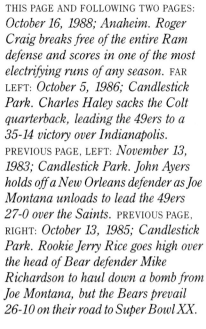

THIS PAGE AND FOLLOWING TWO PAGES: *October 16, 1988; Anaheim. Roger Craig breaks free of the entire Ram defense and scores in one of the most electrifying runs of any season.* FAR LEFT: *October 5, 1986; Candlestick Park. Charles Haley sacks the Colt quarterback, leading the 49ers to a 35-14 victory over Indianapolis.* PREVIOUS PAGE, LEFT: *November 13, 1983; Candlestick Park. John Ayers holds off a New Orleans defender as Joe Montana unloads to lead the 49ers 27-0 over the Saints.* PREVIOUS PAGE, RIGHT: *October 13, 1985; Candlestick Park. Rookie Jerry Rice goes high over the head of Bear defender Mike Richardson to haul down a bomb from Joe Montana, but the Bears prevail 26-10 on their road to Super Bowl XX.*

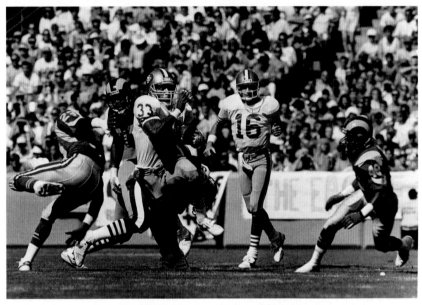

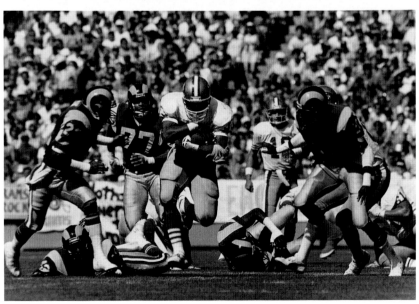

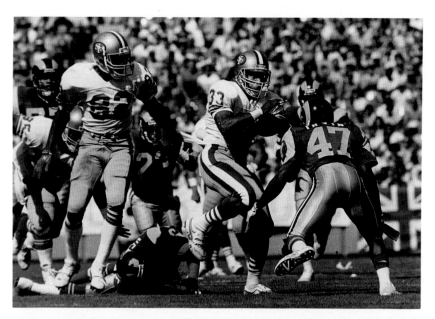

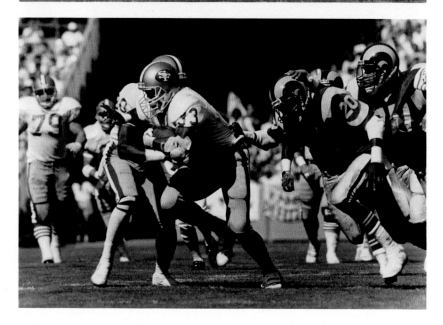

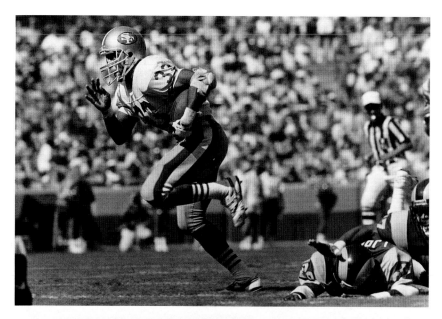

ABOVE: *September 28, 1986; Orange Bowl, Miami. The Good Year blimp hovers overhead while special teams huddle in the steamy sandbox called the Orange Bowl.* RIGHT: *October 9, 1983; Candlestick Park. Linebacker coach Norb Hecker goes over Ram offensive alignments with K.T. (Keena Turner).* FAR RIGHT: *September 3, 1983; Candlestick Park. A concerned Dwight Clark hovers over Joe Montana, who has just been KO'd, as R.C. Owens applies ice to his neck.*

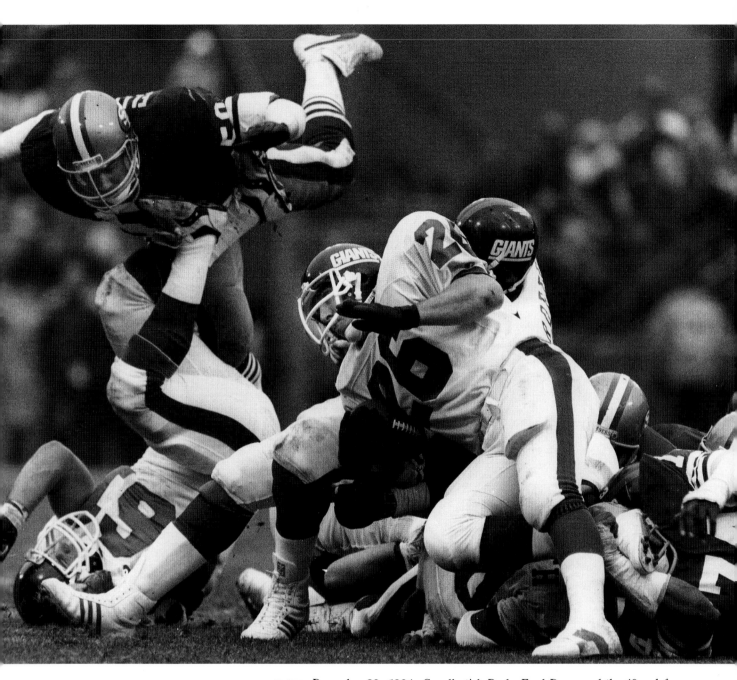

ABOVE: *December 29, 1984; Candlestick Park. Fred Dean and the 49er defense shut down Rob Carpenter and the New York Giants in the divisional play-off. Riki Ellison takes the high road.* LEFT: *January 20, 1985; Super Bowl XIX; Stanford. Wendell Tyler and Roger Craig bask in the glow of a big first-half lead.*

September 30, 1984; Candlestick Park. Ronnie Lott and Jim Stuckey slam Gerald Riggs to the turf. BELOW: *August 15, 1981; Candlestick Park. The first game ever for three 49er rookies who started in the defensive backfield. Left to right, Ronnie Lott, Eric Wright, and Carlton Williamson.* FAR LEFT: *December 22, 1985; Candlestick Park. Michael Carter pushes into the Dallas backfield as the 49ers beat the Cowboys and win the Division.*

October 28, 1984; Anaheim. Riki Ellison and Milt McColl force an Eric Dickerson fumble late in the second quarter to turn the game around for the 49ers. FAR RIGHT: *September 21, 1980; Shea Stadium, New York. Dan Bunz fights off Jet blockers to make tackle in 49er win.*

September 13, 1987; Three River Stadium, Pittsburgh. (Former) defensive line coach Fred vonAppen counsels the defensive line during opening season loss to Pittsburgh. Left to right, Jeff Stover, Kevin Fagan, Michael Carter, Dwaine Board. RIGHT: *November 21, 1988; Candlestick Park. Eyes wide as saucers, Jesse Sapolu prepares to pass-block.*

Randy Cross

Starting in 1976 when he made the All-Rookie team, Randy Cross was regarded as one of the top players in the league; he was named All-Pro in the 49ers' first two Super Bowl seasons and was the 49ers' Offensive Lineman of the Year, 1986-88.

Cross started his career at center, which was also his college position. He moved to guard in 1979, Bill Walsh's first year as coach of the 49ers, and was moved back to center midway through the '87 season when Fred Quillan was injured. Randy stayed at center for his final season in '88. He announced his retirement during Super Bowl week in Miami. He is now a partner in the EC&M advertising firm in Los Gatos and also works on football telecasts.

In addition to his playing ability, Cross was also highly regarded for his leadership and his role as a team spokes-man; he was known as the "Designated Speaker" by the media.

■ My first year with the club was really a pretty good one, under Monte Clark. We lost some tough games because of kicking problems in mid-season and we went downhill after that, but we still finished 8-6.

The next two years we really went downhill. That '78 team was arguably the worst team in the history of the franchise and may have been one of the 10 all-time worst teams in NFL history. I was almost glad that I was on injured reserve because of a broken ankle for the last half of the season.

More than the games, I remember the players from that era because we had some real characters on that team, guys like Cedrick Hardman, Willie Harper, Ralph McGill. We had a defensive back, Mel Morgan, who used to coat his ankles with a mixture of Mississippi mud and vinegar. He said it "pulled out all of the poisons" from his system. He didn't shower after games, either. We had a lot of fun. It didn't come across that way on the field but then, most of our fun was off the field.

When Bill Walsh came to the 49ers, he was our fifth head coach in the four years I'd played for the team. But I think all of us sensed that once he came, we were going to be winners. We knew we'd have an effective offense, so we were really just a good defense away from being a good team.

One of the things that helped bring us together was that we put together our offensive line in '79. I moved to guard, which allowed Fred Quillan to come in at center, and John Ayers moved in at the other guard. John had played both defensive line and offensive tackle before that. In fact, I remember a scrimmage from my rookie year when Monte Clark used John at every defensive and offensive line position.

We might have been the most entertaining 2-14 team in NFL history in '79. We were in just about every game. I think our fans were getting optimistic even though we were losing.

During the '80 season, I started to get the feeling that we could be really good. We opened up that season 3-0 and then lost eight games in a row, but as bad as that streak was, we were close to winning in a lot of games. Then, when we won three of the last five, the team got a lot of confidence, especially from the New Orleans game [when

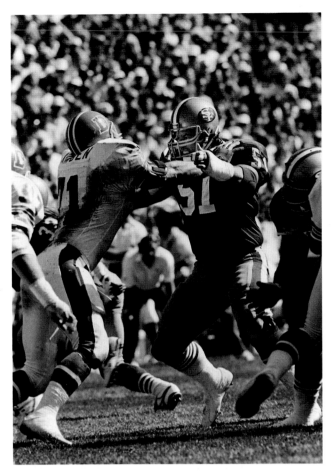

the 49ers, trailing 35-7 at halftime, came back to win, 38-35, in overtime].

I thought we'd have a good year in '81, but nobody could have seen what would happen. I think there were two games midway in that season that showed us we could play with anybody. The Dallas game was one. We were up 21-0 after the first quarter of that game and ended up winning 45-14. Then we went back to Pittsburgh and beat the Steelers. That was when we realized what a good defense we had. We'd had a strong offense in '79; we'd score 30 points a game — but our defense would give up 35. But suddenly we had guys like Carlton Williamson beating up on people, breaking ribs. When you see that happening it makes you play harder on offense.

Joe Montana had taken over at quarterback the back half of the '80 season. Joe's a strange guy in one way. He's not your typical aggressive field general, not a fiery guy like Jim McMahon. But once he stepped into the lineup it was like he'd always been there. We always got a confident feeling because we knew he'd find a way to get the job done.

As special as the three Super Bowls were, they were nothing like the championship game against Dallas that season. As a player, to be in a championship game for the first time was special, and that was probably as exciting a game as I've ever been in. Maybe it was because it was in our home park, maybe it was because we'd accomplished something on a pretty grand scale. People were jumping up

and going crazy, just losing it. I wish you could bottle the emotion in the park that day.

I remember thinking that, because we'd blown the Cowboys out in the regular season, they'd really be up for the game, and they were. But our defense played a very aggressive game, and we moved the ball better than I ever thought we'd be able to against the flex defense. Remember, the Cowboys were in their prime at that time, with guys like Too-Tall Jones, Randy White, and Harvey Martin.

There were a lot of similarities between the '81 team and last year's team. Both teams had some veteran types mixed in with younger fellows.

Last year was special for me because the players actually took charge of the team. When we were 6-5, it was getting to be embarrassing, and that kind of thing is always great motivation. We were having regular team meetings. Basically, the meetings gave people a chance to blow off steam. If players thought that so-and-so wasn't working hard enough on the practice field, they really started speaking up. It was almost a socialist society.

The Super Bowl was special for me, the result more special than the way it was played. I'd always wanted to go out on a winning note. I had actually made up my mind to retire in late September or early October, but I'd been thinking about it for some time. When you get up in age in football, it's tough to relate to the younger players. They have a different attitude toward the game. When you've been on a winning team, it's hard to imagine that there are players who won't do everything it takes to win.

There was an episode in London when we were there to play an exhibition game. I was talking to Merlin Olsen, and when he left, a younger player said to me, "Do you know Father Murphy?" One of the greatest players of all time, and this kid knew Merlin only as a TV character.

As the final game of my career the last Super Bowl is certainly a great highlight, but frankly, I was a little frustrated with the game because I think it was obvious that we were the better team. We should have scored three touchdowns in the first half and maybe another three in the second. It should have been one of those ugly Super Bowls instead of the great one it became. It's to the Bengals' credit that they made it a close game.

I've practiced selective blocking with that game, so I don't remember a low snap on a field goal attempt or getting called for holding. Anyway, in 10 years I'm sure I'll look back and remember it as a game where I played incredibly well.

Jerry Rice

Jerry Rice may be the most dominating offensive player in the NFL. Though he's playing in a quarterback-focused game, he has won the Most Valuable Player award for a season (1987) and for the 49ers' third Super Bowl win, on January 23, 1989.

Rice set a team record in his rookie year (1985) with 241 receiving yards on 10 catches in a game against the Los Angeles Rams, and he set team season records the following year with 1,570 receiving yards and 16 touchdown receptions.

That was just a warm-up for 1987, when Rice set NFL records for receiving touchdowns (22, despite missing four games because of that year's strike) and consecutive games (13) in which he scored on a pass reception.

An ankle injury slowed Rice for much of the '88 season,

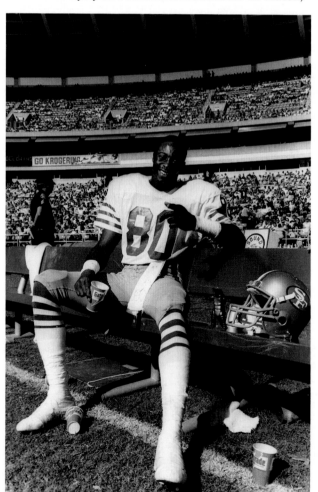

but he reached peak form again in the post-season.

In the first playoff game against Minnesota he caught three touchdown passes from Joe Montana in a surprisingly lopsided 34-9 win. On a bitterly cold day in Chicago he got the 49ers rolling with a 61-yard touchdown in the first quarter and added a 27-yard TD reception in the second quarter, allowing the 49ers to sweep by the Bears, 28-3, in the NFC championship game. Finally, he tied another Super Bowl record with 215 receiving yards on 11 catches. He caught the first touchdown pass for the 49ers in that game and set up the winning score with a 27-yard pass on third-and-20 from the Cincinnati 45.

■ When I came to the 49ers in 1985 they had just won the Super Bowl, so I figured we'd be right back the next year and I'd get my ring. But it didn't work out that way. We didn't make it for my first three years, and I was beginning to think I'd never play in a Super Bowl.

That's why this last season was such a great experience for me. When you haven't gone to a Super Bowl you really appreciate the chance to play in one. It was nice to break the records in '87, but we lost in the playoffs, so it was a disappointing year for me overall. When you have a great season and a great post-season it's much more fulfilling.

The year before I was really fatigued at the end. I just couldn't do the things I wanted to do. Last year I think the ankle injury really helped me in a way, because I was totally rested going into the playoffs. I really felt good.

The Super Bowl was a great experience, something I'll remember the rest of my life. I'll especially remember that last drive. When Joe came into the huddle at the start of that drive it was so quiet. You could have heard a pin drop on the grass. But Joe had that look in his eyes, and we knew we were going to win the game.

The one play I remember most is the pass over the middle [to the Cincinnati 18]. When I caught the ball, I turned up field and I really thought I was going to score. I don't know how [Lewis] Billups made the tackle. John Taylor was trying to block him, but Billups still got me. But it turned out all right because we scored a couple of plays later. It was a frustrating game in a way because it took us so long to score a touchdown, but when we won everything was fine.

There's only one thing wrong with being in the Super Bowl—it sure shortens the off-season. It seems like we just finished playing and we had to go back to work again.

When I first came to the 49ers I just wanted to be able to make a contribution. I was surprised that I got a chance to start right away because I knew Freddy Solomon was here, and he'd really been a good receiver for the team.

Then it didn't work out right at first. I had a lot of problems. I just didn't feel confident out there. The system was so complex, and I was having to think about what I was doing all the time instead of just playing. I was dropping a lot of passes, and I'd never had that trouble before. Me, dropping passes? I couldn't believe it. But I couldn't really focus on what I was doing.

But I finally got there. After the Rams game I felt very comfortable when I came to the line of scrimmage, and now I think I have a real good concept of the offense. I don't have to stop to think about what I'm doing all the time, and that's taken a lot of pressure off me. I just play football.

The records are nice, but that's not what I play football for. I want to win. In fact, the year I set all the records I tried each week not to think about them. I put them out of my mind. I was just trying to play hard and have fun.

That's why I never set personal goals for myself. I have just one goal for myself, and that's to be considered one of the best receivers of all time. I know I have to play several

years like I'm playing now to be in that category, but I think I can. I think I'm still improving. I don't think I've reached my peak yet.

I've learned a lot more about the game since I've been here. In college I could just use my physical ability. Now I like to study the films to see what defenses do against other teams. That gives me an idea how they'll react against me.

I like to experiment in the games. I'll show the defensive backs some moves just to see how they react. If the ball is going to the other side, I'll still make my moves and watch the DBs. Then, when the ball comes my way, I know exactly what to expect from them.

There's a lot of communication on the sidelines with me and Joe and Bill [Walsh]. I'll tell them how the DBs are playing me and what I think I can do. But I never tell Bill, "I'll just go 20 yards down the field and have Joe throw the ball to me." I used to do that in college. I'd tell the coach that I was open for a certain type of play. Then the quarterback would throw the pass and it would be intercepted. So that taught me a lesson.

It's been great playing for Bill. He's got such a great mind for the game of football. He knows how to utilize everybody. Other teams can't focus on just one guy because there's something different going on all the time. I'm almost always in motion to one side or the other, so they can't predict that I'll be going one way all the time. And Bill changes the game plans all the time, so other teams never know exactly how to prepare for us.

Bill treats you like a man, with respect. I've seldom seen him lose his composure, maybe once or twice at most. A lot of coaches get ticked off and start yelling at players, but Bill's not that type. I think that's why the players all respect him.

And we know what we're going to do at the start of the game because he writes down the first 25 plays. That's great because you can take the plays and study them the night before the game. So when the game starts, there's no hesitation. You know exactly what you're supposed to be doing.

I've really enjoyed playing for the 49ers, and I enjoy this area. I went back to Mississippi after my first season, but I've lived out here year-round since then.

I think we all get along really well, but it's not a matter of hanging out with each other so much. I think about 90 percent of the team is married, so when practice is over we go home to our families. It's a very businesslike operation.

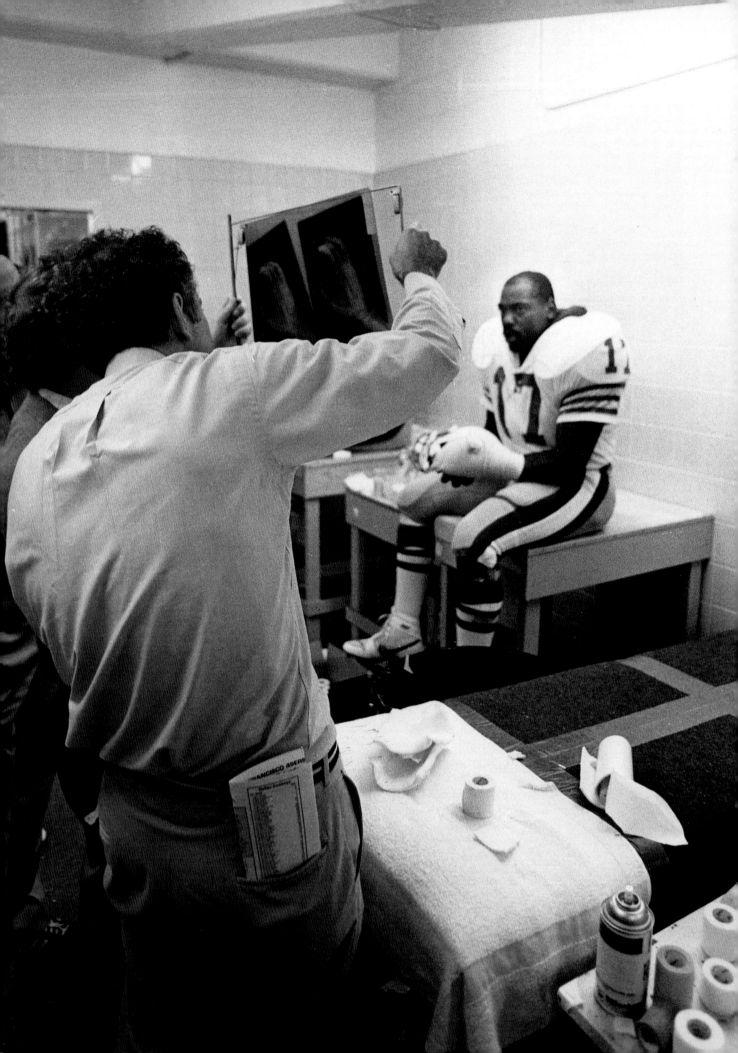

Halftime

RIGHT: *September 28, 1986; Orange Bowl, Miami. Defensive coordinator George Seifert meets in a humid halftime locker room with Tim McKyer, Ronnie Lott, and Carlton Williamson.* BELOW: *January 10, 1982; NFC Championship; Candlestick Park. Joe Montana stares ahead as Dwight Clark sneaks a look at plays on the blackboard. The 49ers won, 28-27. The board behind Joe was signed by each member of the team and was displayed in the locker room at practice and at the stadium the day of the game.* PREVIOUS PAGE, LEFT: *August 22, 1987; Candlestick Park. Team doctor Michael Dillingham examines an X-ray of Kevin Dean.* PREVIOUS PAGE, RIGHT: *October 12, 1986; Candlestick Park. Bill Walsh goes over last-minute offensive adjustments as the 49ers prepare to take the field for the third quarter. Left to right: Dwight Clark, Jeff Kemp, Mike Moroski, Mike Wilson, Mike Holmgren, and Jerry Rice.*

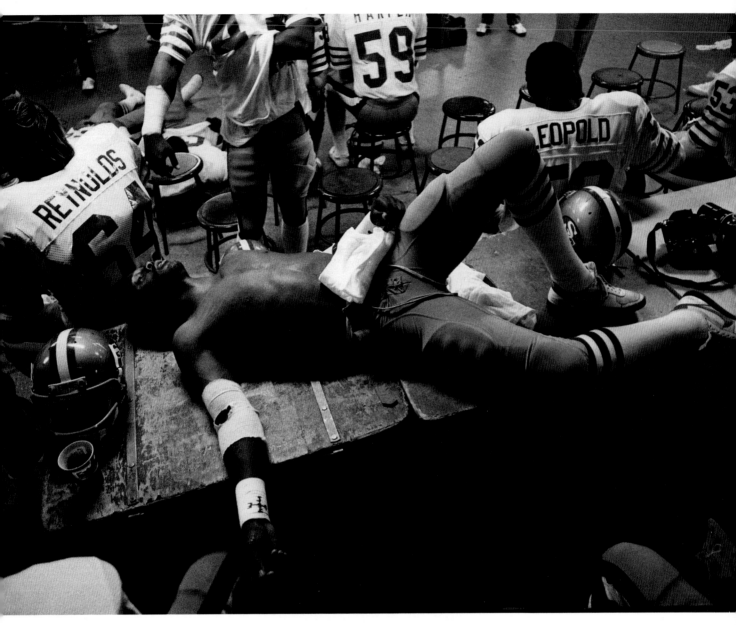

ABOVE: *September 18, 1983; Busch Stadium, St. Louis. With field temperatures reaching 110 degrees and the Astroturf reflecting heat like a griddle, the 49er locker room at halftime resembled a Turkish sauna. Eric Wright stretches out.*

November 1, 1987; Anaheim. Lindsy McLean stretching Roger Craig between halves of 49ers 31-10 win over the Rams. LEFT: *October 25, 1987; Superdome, New Orleans. Russ Francis applies ice before the 49ers retake the field and defeat the Saints 24-22.*

ABOVE: *October 8, 1984; Meadowlands, New York. Coach Walsh goes over changes with the team at halftime in the 49ers' Monday night win over the Giants. Bob McKittrick, offensive line coach, looks on.* RIGHT: *September 28, 1986; Orange Bowl, Miami. Brothers-in-law Max Runager and Ray Wersching try to cool off in the 49er locker room at halftime.* LEFT: *October 14, 1984; Candlestick Park. Trainer Lindsy McLean tapes Wendell Tyler at halftime during the 49ers only season loss to the Steelers.*

PROFILE

Jack Reynolds

Jack (Hacksaw) Reynolds, who played on the 1981 and 1984 Super Bowl teams, was easily the most colorful of all the 49ers of the Walsh years.

Reynolds got his nickname in college at Tennessee. Upset because Ol' Miss had demolished the Vols, 38-0, to prevent Tennessee from going to the Sugar Bowl, Reynolds bought a hacksaw and sawed a motorless 1953 Chevy in half, a job which took a day and a half.

Jack was known for his dedication to the game, to the point of putting on his uniform hours before the game. He had a garage full of notes on defensive opponents and was truly a coach on the field, particularly for the youthful '81 team, which was Reynolds's ninth straight play-off team.

As the middle linebacker in the 4-3 defense, Reynolds

called defensive signals. His most famous call came against Cincinnati in the 49ers' first Super Bowl. The Bengals had fourth-and-goal on the San Francisco one and Reynolds called the defense that stopped the Bengals cold, a key play in the 49ers' ultimate 26-21 victory.

Reynolds now splits his time between southern California, Miami and San Salvador island in the Bahamas.

■ We had played Cincinnati in December '81 and beat them, but we couldn't stop [fullback] Pete Johnson at all. He averaged seven yards a carry. During the game, our defensive line coach, Bill McPherson, told me, "I see something, but I don't want you to use it in this game because we might play these guys again." And sure enough, we played the Bengals in the Super Bowl, so Bill's remark was pretty prophetic.

Johnson lined up in a right-handed stance. When his left arm was draped loosely over his knee, he wasn't going to get the ball. When he had his left elbow in tight against his body, he was going to get the ball. I played off that the whole game. I was the only one who knew about it. McPherson told me, "Don't tell any of the others because it'll just confuse them."

When we were in that goal line stand (in the third quarter), on fourth down I looked into the backfield and the other back, Charles Alexander, was cheated toward the line of scrimmage and Johnson had his left elbow tight against his body. So I figured Alexander was going to be the lead blocker and Johnson was going to carry the ball. I figured that was the time to gamble, and it turned out I was right. But it was the defensive line that really made that play. If the line doesn't hold, the linebackers can't make tackles.

I remember Bill Walsh had rock music playing while we were practicing because we'd be playing in an indoor stadium where the noise can really be overwhelming. That really helped us get ready for the crowd noise. It was a pro-Cincinnati radio station, too, so that worked even more to our advantage.

There was one other thing I think made a difference. I knew it would be a zoo going in, and it was worse because [then Vice President George] Bush's motorcade held everything up. That didn't bother us a lot, but I think that really shook up Cincinnati. The Bengals didn't seem ready for the game to start.

I had the unique experience of playing both for and

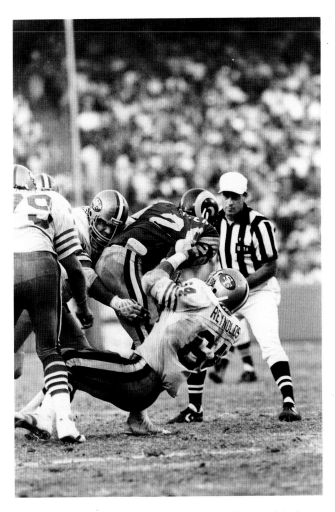

exciting Super Bowls ever. To tell you the truth, I don't think either team played very well this year. The difference was Joe Montana, but it's always been that way. As Joe Montana goes, so go the 49ers, at least offensively.

I knew how lucky we were that year. A lot of things went right for us and we won a lot of games just on Ray Wersching's foot. But we had one thing going for us: we all respected each other. When I was with the Rams they used to talk about being one big happy family, but they preached one thing and practiced another. With the 49ers we really acted that way. We didn't all like each other, but we had respect, which is the important thing.

And, of course, it went just the other way in '82, but that didn't surprise me. We knew how fragile we were. We had just 11 starters on offense and defense, no depth at all. So when we had injuries we didn't have anybody left.

I was one of the few players on the '81 team with play-off experience, and I'd had a ton of it, so I was a coach on the field that year but, hell, I was a coach for the Rams, too. I've always been very motivated. Most players aren't. It really burns me up to see players who don't work hard to be the best. If you're a good player, why not try to be great? If I'd been tall and fast I could have been a better player, but I think I made the most out of what I had.

I used to be famous for wearing my uniform to the stadium, but there was a good reason for that. I didn't like to get to the stadium and then have to wait around with everybody else to be taped. I wanted to be ready to go when I got there.

That actually started with the Rams. I'd get up early, eat early; I couldn't eat with the team because I was so emotional, I'd get sick. Then I'd get taped and put on my uniform. On the road I'd even go to church in my uniform.

Usually I took a taxi to the game, although I did ride once on the team bus because I wanted to get there early. I loved being at the stadium at 9:30 for a one o'clock game. For home games I had my own car. I'd be driving down the freeway and people would think I was just another one of those fans who liked to dress up in a team uniform. They thought I was just another nut. Little did they know, I really was a nut.

The remarkable thing about the Bill Walsh years is that the 49ers have won three Super Bowls in eight years. I think it's a lot harder to win these days because there's so much balance. When I came into the game in the '70s, I remember Dallas and Pittsburgh and Miami were so dominant, but now they're down and the 49ers have stayed up there.

against Bill Walsh. I knew from my experience with the Rams that he had a great offense.

I had problems with the Rams ever since my contract dispute with them in '77. They tried to trade me to Tampa Bay that year, figuring they were sending me to Outer Mongolia. That was fine with me, but when I got to Tampa Bay, I said I wanted my contract renegotiated because I'd have to play three seasons in one since they were such a bad team. So they sent me back to the Rams.

In '81 the Rams decided they wouldn't pick up my option. They told me I was through as a player. Well, I had just been to the pro Bowl the year before, so I couldn't have been too bad.

I was going to Buffalo when I got a call from Bill Walsh, and I decided to go to the 49ers. It cost me $85,000 in base salary, but money isn't the only thing that motivates me.

No, I didn't think we'd win a championship in '81. I don't think anybody did, even Bill. I think he kept expecting something to go wrong. The 49ers were 6-10 the year before and we went 13-3 that year. That just doesn't happen in the NFL.

The funny thing is, Cincinnati did the same thing. They hadn't done anything the year before, and all of a sudden they were in the Super Bowl too. I thought about that this year watching the Super Bowl — the same two teams. And the '81 game and this year's were probably the two most

Keith Fahnhorst

Keith Fahnhorst was drafted out of the University of Minnesota on the second round in 1974 as a tight end. Shifted to offensive tackle early in his rookie year, Fahnhorst became a bulwark in the offensive line. A pinched nerve in his neck caused his retirement after the 1987 season, but by that time he had outplayed every other player in the 49ers' 1974 draft by at least five years. He played in the first two of the 49ers' three Super Bowls and formed a brother team with linebacker Jim Fahnhorst for the 1984 championship team.

A leader on the field, Fahnhorst was also a leader away from the field. When Skip Vanderbundt was traded to New Orleans in 1977, Keith became the club's player representative, a position he held during the NFL players' strikes in 1982 and 1987. His leadership helped hold the 49ers

together in '87, a year in which they had the league's best season record, 13-2.

Fahnhorst is now a stockbroker with Dain Bosworth in Minneapolis and also works part-time as a players' agent.

■ I played a few games as a tight end in my rookie season. I think I caught one pass for one yard. Obviously I wasn't in there for my receiving ability: I was there to block. Sure, I was disappointed when I was moved to tackle. I still have a picture somewhere of me with "89" (a receiver's number) on my uniform. I thought it would be easy to play tackle. All you had to do was shuffle your feet a little and block. I found out it ain't that easy. But though I was disappointed that I was moved, there's no question it really extended my career. I would never have lasted that long as a tight end.

Dick Nolan was my first coach in 1974. After that there was a bunch of them until Bill Walsh came in '79.

I don't have any specific memories of the bad years; I've blotted them all out. What I remember most is how we looked forward to the off-season, just getting out of there. It wasn't much fun. We were getting beat all the time and we didn't have much fan support.

But I think those of us who went through the bad years had more of an appreciation for the good years when they came. A lot of players never have anything but losing seasons in their careers. In my first seven years, we had only one winning season (8-6 in 1976), and when we had those consecutive 2-14 seasons in '78 and '79, I didn't know if we'd ever see the light at the end of the tunnel, let alone a championship.

It's a lot different for the young players joining the team now. As soon as they put on that uniform they're 49ers, and they're looked on as part of a championship team, even though they've never played in a Super Bowl. I'm sure it's exciting for them when they win, but it can never be as thrilling as it was for those of us who survived the bad years.

The most thrilling season, no question, was 1981. I guess you can never duplicate the excitement of that first win, and this was doubly exciting because it was so unexpected. I know I didn't expect it. All I was hoping for that year was that we'd have a winning season. We'd only been 6-10 the previous season.

A lot of things came together that year. We were lucky because we were able to avoid injuries to key players. Joe

Montana really came into his own that year, and Dwight Clark had a great year too. And we had a lot of closeness on that team, everybody pulling together. That helped get us through the tough spots that you have in any season, even a championship one.

The most memorable game that season — and the most memorable game of my entire career — was the championship game against Dallas. Just the fact that we were even in that position made it special, and then the way the game went — that last drive, "The Catch" by Dwight. It was a storybook end to a storybook season. You couldn't have written a script like that.

The best team I played on, though, was the 1984 team. There was just so much talent on that team. Fred Dean was at his best that year, and we were just solid everywhere. And there was a great deal of mutual respect on that team, just like '81, and that helped us ride out the potential problems.

We knew going into the season that we had the best team and that if we just stayed halfway healthy we should win it. Of course you still have to prove it on the field, and we did that. That team played so consistently all the way through the season and the Super Bowl. Our win over Miami in the Super Bowl was about as good a game as I ever played in. We just did everything right that day.

The next season [when the 49ers fell to 10-6 and lost to the Giants in the wild card play-off game] was a real disappointment. People say that a team gets complacent after it wins, that players aren't as "hungry" as they were the season before, but I don't think that happened to us. We always had a very professional approach to the game — we trained very hard, for instance. We weren't about to be complacent.

If anything, I think we may have tried too hard. We put a lot of extra pressure on ourselves. We were trying to think back to what we'd done the year before, when we'd won, and trying to do the same thing, but it wasn't so easy the second time around.

The biggest factor, I think, was that everybody was gunning for us. We wanted to win just as much as we had the year before, but other teams wanted to beat us even more than they had. It's tougher, too, because your season is longer when you win the Super Bowl, and it's harder to come back mentally at the start of the next season. And there are always a lot of distractions when you're a champion.

I think the thing I remember most about playing for the 49ers during the championship years was the closeness of the team. That helped us survive the strike in '87.

I'd been the player rep. during the first strike and I'd learned my lesson; I resigned after that year. But when Bill Ring retired, that left the job open again and I took it. The strike could have divided the team because there were some players who had crossed the picket lines [to play in the replacement games] and some who stayed out. There was the potential for holding grudges. But we talked out our differences when we all came back, and we were able to put that all behind us. Of course it helped that we had been a winning team and we knew we had to pull together to win again, but the big thing was that we had been friends and we didn't want to lose that feeling.

I made some real friends on the team. One from the early days was Paul Hofer. I was really disappointed that Paul couldn't play on our '81 team [Hofer was on injured reserve for the year]. He'd pretty much carried the team in the lean years, but his knee injury forced him to retire that season. I didn't think that was fair, but I guess there are a lot of things in football that aren't fair.

Randy Cross, John Ayers, and Fred Quillan became good friends because we played together all those years. We went through the rough times together and reaped the benefits of the good years, so we became special friends.

2nd Half

October 18, 1981; County Stadium, Wisconsin. Paul Hofer, two-time Eshmont Award winner and perennial 110 percenter, sweeps end against Green Bay. The Eshmont is given to the player voted by the team to be most valuable in ability and/or inspiration. LEFT: *November 25, 1979; Candlestick Park. An anguished Bill Walsh moments after a DeBerg interception kills the 49er hopes against the Rams.* PREVIOUS PAGE, LEFT: *December 14, 1986; Sullivan Stadium, Massachusetts. Jeff Fuller returns an interception, highlighting a great game for him and the entire 49er defense. He is flanked by Keena Turner and Ronnie Lott.* PREVIOUS PAGE, RIGHT: *December 14, 1986; Sullivan Stadium, Massachusetts. As Fred Quillan blocks, Joe Montana hits Jerry Rice in the cold and snow of a New England winter.*

January 10, 1982; Candlestick Park.
Dwight Clark is up-ended early in the
fourth quarter of the 49er championship
win over Dallas. In the background,
Bill Ring takes out two cowboy
pursuers. FAR RIGHT: *September 22,*
1985; Los Angeles Coliseum. Mike
Walter and Riki Ellison celebrate after
Milt McColl (53) takes a turnover in
for a score against the Raiders.

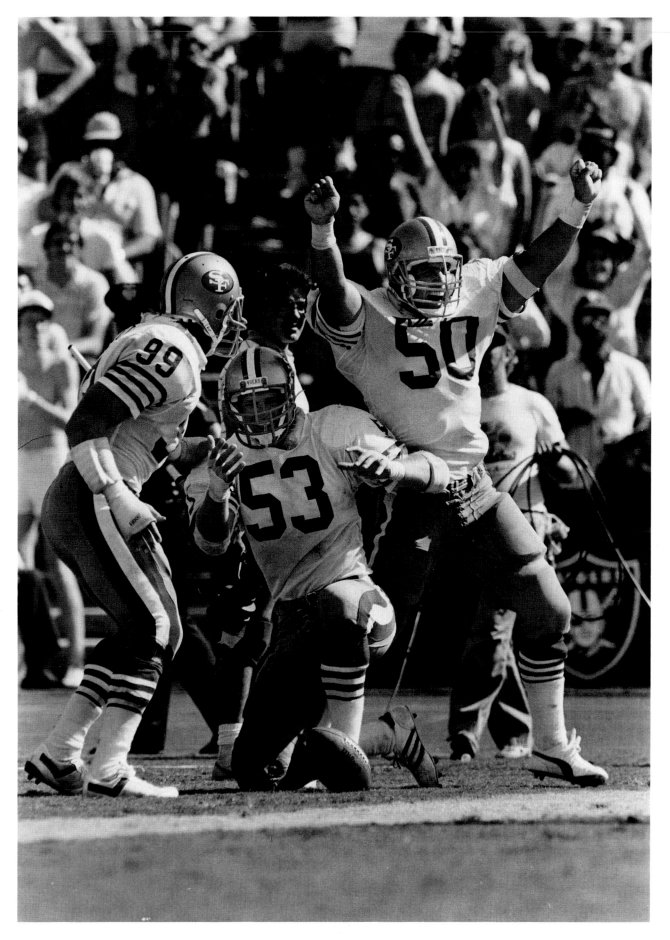

ABOVE: *January 8, 1989; NFC Championship; Soldier Field, Chicago. Forty Niner players huddle for warmth in the arctic chill of a Midwest winter. The 49ers won 28-3.* RIGHT: *December 9, 1979; Candlestick Park. Chico Norton, equipment manager, 1979. Chico has been with the 49ers since 1955, longer than any other employee. Up to that point the Niners had never won a Championship.* LEFT: *November 2, 1980; Silverdome, Pontiac, Michigan. Charle Young heads up field, but the 49ers fall short against Detroit. Young brought veteran stability to the young 49ers and helped lead the team to their first Super Bowl a year later.*

January 22, 1989; Super Bowl XXIII; Miami, Florida. Kevin Fagan, Charles Haley, and Mike Walter surround Bengal quarterback Boomer Esiason. RIGHT: *December 8, 1984; Candlestick Park. Dana McLemore breaks a punt return for big yardage in the rain as the 49ers paste the Vikings 51-7.*

September 23, 1984; Veterans Stadium, Philadelphia. Keith Fahnhorst comes out to embrace his brother Jim, whose fourth-quarter interception ices a victory over the Eagles. Carlton Williamson (27) looks on. BELOW: *October 4, 1981; RFK Stadium, Washington, DC. Larry Pillers, Paul Hofer, Archie Reese, and Dwaine Board congratulate Dwight Hicks after he returned his second interception of the day for a touchdown, helping the 49ers defeat the Redskins.*

September 22, 1985; Los Angeles Coliseum. Nowhere to run, nowhere to hide: Marcus Allen surrounded by 49er defenders, left to right, Jeff Stover, Manu Tuiasosopo, Carlton Williamson, Todd Shell, Mike Walter, Riki Ellison, and Ronnie Lott.

December 1, 1986; Candlestick Park. Mark Bavaro drags Ronnie Lott, Keena Turner, and the entire 49er defense along in the third quarter, spearheading the Giants to a come-from-behind win on a Monday night and vaulting them into the Super Bowl. RIGHT: *December 6, 1981; Riverfront Stadium, Cincinnati. Fashion-plate punter Jim Miller surveys the field during a 49er win over the Bengals in frosty Cincinnati.*

*September 8, 1983; Minneapolis,
Minnesota. Eric Wright celebrates on
the sidelines after his third interception
in a big win (48-17) over the Vikings.*
BELOW: *October 2, 1988; Candlestick
Park. John Taylor's explosive punt
return for a touchdown leads the 49ers
over Detroit 20-13.*

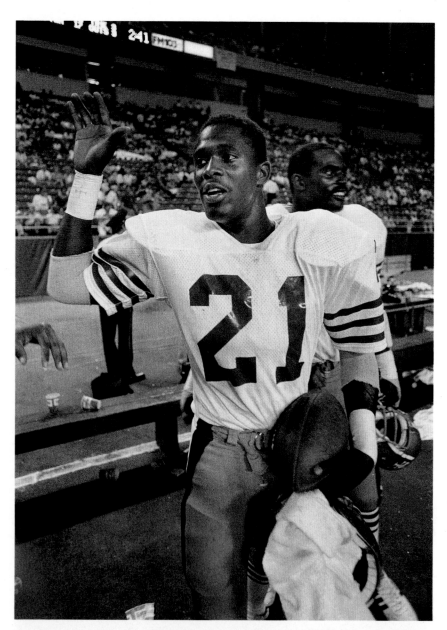

January 6, 1985; NFC Championship; Candlestick Park. Hacksaw Reynolds, on-field defense architect, studies Chicago formations with Keena Turner.

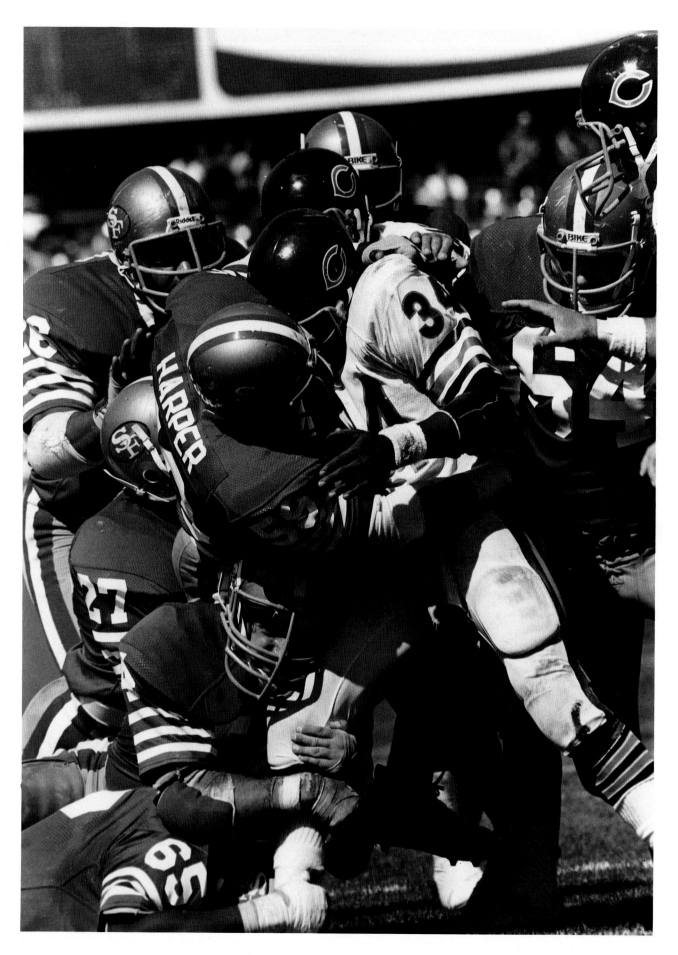

November 8, 1981; Candlestick Park. Freddie Solomon, the "Linkster" to his teammates, pulls in a touchdown pass to help the Niners beat the tough Atlanta Falcons. RIGHT: *November 18, 1984; Candlestick Park. Defensive coach Bill McPherson and assistant defensive coach and former 49er great Tommy Hart counsel the defensive line in 49er win over Tampa Bay.* LEFT: *September 13, 1981; Candlestick Park. Willie Harper (59) and Hacksaw Reynolds (64) lead the defense as the 49ers open the season by stopping Walter Payton of the Chicago Bears.*

January 24, 1982; Super Bowl XVI; Pontiac, Michigan. The goal-line stand that assures a Super Bowl win. Forty Niners hold Bengals four times from the one. Final score: 26-21. RIGHT: *November 22, 1981; Anaheim. Ray Wersching's last-second 49-yard field goal beats the Rams 33-31.*

Dwight Clark

Dwight Clark is one of the great NFL success stories. Looking for a quarterback, Bill Walsh had gone to Clemson to watch Steve Fuller work out. Walsh wasn't impressed by Fuller, but he liked what he saw of Clark, on the receiving end of Fuller's passes, and drafted him.

Clark may have been the best 10th round pick ever. He set 49er records with 506 catches and 6,750 receiving yards before his 1988 retirement, but he is best known for "The Catch," the touchdown against Dallas in the NFC championship game after the '81 season, a play which is still regarded as one of the 10 most exciting in NFL history.

Clark was a very deceptive receiver. He wasn't fast but he had a knack for getting open, and when defensive backs came up to shut off short passes he'd go by them for a long one. He caught 48 touchdowns in his career, third best in 49er history, and had one for 80 yards. Bigger than most wide receivers, he punished defensive backs with his blocking.

Always very popular with his teammates, Dwight

received the Len Eshmont Award in 1982. He now co-owns one restaurant with several teammates, and owns another, Clark's by the Bay, in Redwood City.

■ I didn't expect to be around long. I thought I'd just go out to California to the mini-camp and see what happened. I got a $5,000 signing bonus, which was great. If I made the team I'd get $30,000, which is a lot of money in South Carolina.

I took my golf clubs to camp. I thought if I got cut after a couple of weeks I'd just go on down the coast and play Pebble Beach and maybe some courses in Santa Barbara and L.A. and then fly home. I thought I'd never get a chance to go back to California.

Once I made the team I was still shocked. That was the year we had like 32 defensive backs, bringing in people all the time, so I thought, "What's to keep them from bringing in 32 wide receivers?" As the season went on I thought, "I've made it through half a season," then three-quarters of a season. I was just happy to be here.

Even in training camp the next season I didn't think I'd stick. But I had some success that second year. I remember I caught six passes against New Orleans, which was a big deal; I had only caught 33 passes my entire college career. So I felt the next year I had my foot in the door.

During the Jets game that second season I caught two touchdown passes, my first as a pro. I never thought of having so much ability, but I just fit into Bill's system so well. I did what I was told. Those touchdowns, it was just like Bill wrote it. I cut in, then cut out and left the guy right there. I caught that second touchdown and I spiked the ball. I thought, "This is it, I've got it made." Then when I trotted off and hit the track around Shea Stadium I slid right on my butt. The New York fans loved it. They got a good laugh.

I hated watching films. Out of the 9 years I played I can't count 10 times I learned something on the films. I had to do it on the field against the scout team using the defense of the team we'd be playing that week. My whole career, Joe [Montana] and I would stay out on the field after practice and work on things. I'm not a natural athlete. If I'm going to be good at something I have to do it over and over again. I'm not like Jerry Rice, who is so gifted.

Jerry is undoubtedly the best I've ever seen. He's got the work ethic of Bill Ring and he's got all the talent. He amazes me. I've never seen anybody go to the ball like he

The Catch was the biggest exclamation point in an incredible season. The Super Bowl was an anticlimax after that. The fans here wanted to beat Dallas so bad. When I played against them one time I hated the Cowboys as much as the fans did. They were such cocky guys. And I played on a couple of teams when they just beat us to death.

To beat them at their own game, to come back and beat them the way they'd beaten the 49ers [in playoffs in the early '70s], it was just too much. This city went berserk. It wasn't just The Catch. It was all those years of frustration.

The 1981 season was destiny. It was such a surprise every week. Guys would ask me, "Are you guys really that good?" I'd say that I didn't know. We'd been losers forever, 2-14 two years in a row, 6-10 that second year I was here. Then all of a sudden we'd come into the locker room winners week after week.

The Pittsburgh game was the real turnaround. We not only beat them but we got behind and came back and beat a team that had been World Champions four times. I could remember Bill Walsh jumping up and down in the locker room.

That's the most fun I've had in my life, the plane ride home. You'd think we'd have been tired, but it was like a party.

The '84 season wasn't even close to the same feeling. We had 49 guys on the roster, and all 49 players did something to help us win. We were so deep it didn't matter who got hurt. We'd go out on the field and just methodically beat everybody.

Winning the Super Bowl any time is the greatest thing you can ever do, but that first year the fans didn't expect it and they were so pumped up. The second time they expected us to win. We had the best players, the best coach, the best owner.

Plus, in '81 I had a lot more to do with it. In '84 I contributed, but we had Roger Craig, Wendell Tyler, Russ Francis — we had a lot of weapons.

When I retired I thought about going back to South Carolina and buying a big farm, but I like California. There's nothing like the Bay Area. This is like the second part of my life. I've got a lot of ties here. I have a lot of friends, probably more than I do at home. California, especially the Bay Area, is the best place to live.

I miss being one of the guys. It's such a close-knit group. Once that game starts it's like being in a war. To have those guys in your corner was so sweet. I knew John Ayers or Keith Fahnhorst would always back me up if I got in trouble. Russ Francis is an independent guy, but when you're on the field he's there. I knew that any time I got into a fight he'd be right there, and he's the kind of guy you want to have there.

I miss going out there and doing something that's good. It's a little different when you go from "Boy, that was a great move you put on that guy" to "Boy, the sauce you put on that pepper steak was great." It doesn't get the same effect.

does. He just sees the ball and gets it. I've heard Bill tell Joe, "If you get in trouble, just throw it in Jerry's direction and he'll get it." And he does. The ball looks like it's 10 yards downfield and he'll get it.

The coaching I got from Bill and Sam Wyche the first few years I really locked into. What Bill had to say and all his experience as a coach, and Sam Wyche's ability to get his point across from his playing experience — those two guys are really what got my career going.

Part of the reason I made the team was the "Charlie Hustle" type of attitude I had that was instilled in me at Clemson. When I got to camp I was going downfield blocking guys and, as a borderline case, that helped keep me around.

The Catch was like the greatest thing that could happen to me in life. You only get two or three chances in life to do something that makes a great impact, and I think I was just so fortunate to be in a position to take advantage of it. It could easily have been a drop.

I'm sure there are guys who have had good careers but because they haven't done things like The Catch, or Steve Young's great run, or Joe's great drives, they won't be remembered as much.

I kind of dig the notoriety part of it. I get the perfect amount of notoriety. I don't get bombarded like Joe Montana, who gets it all the time. I get enough, it strokes my ego a little bit but doesn't bug me to death. I'm kind of a people person anyway. I like to talk to people.

Keena Turner

Keena Turner was drafted by the 49ers in 1980 and became a full-time starter at outside linebacker in '81, the first of the 49ers' Super Bowl years. Keena excels at all phases of the game: in 1984 he tied with Ronnie Lott for the team lead in interceptions, four; in 1985 he tied for the team lead in fumble recoveries, two; in 1986 he tied for the team lead with four forced fumbles and led the linebackers in sacks for the second straight year.

Turner was chosen by his teammates to receive the Len Eshmont Award for "courageous and inspirational play" in 1984.

Turner and Eric Wright are co-founders of Champs Foundation, a scholarship program for Bay Area student-athletes. He and Wright are co-owners with Lott, Roger Craig, Carlton Williamson, and Dwight Clark of the Sports City Cafe, a restaurant in Cupertino.

■ I knew so little about the 49ers when I was drafted that I didn't even know who the coach was. I had been contacted by Norb Hecker, and I thought he was the head coach. I was just happy I was going somewhere warm and where they played on grass. Other than that, I didn't know

what to expect.

I had mostly thought in terms of Minnesota and Green Bay when I was growing up because those were the teams my dad followed, and when I visited Minnesota before the draft I was impressed with their operation and their coaches. Even though I grew up in Chicago [and graduated from the same high school as Dick Butkus], we didn't follow the Bears for some reason. And I never wanted to play for the Bears because I'm not a fan of playing on artificial turf.

When I came here I was fortunate that the 49ers had players like Charle Young and Willie Harper, who guided me along. That first year I mostly played behind Harper, and really, for the first part of the season, I was just trying to prove myself worthy of playing on the team. That was my total focus. I didn't think much about the team until later.

But that second year there was a lot more talent, with guys like Ronnie Lott and Fred Dean coming in. Nobody expected us to do much, but we had the attitude that, if we worked hard enough, we'd win. We still didn't have a whole lot of talent, but we played together.

The first Dallas game was the one that made me think we could be a championship team. We had been winning a lot of real close games but not blowing anybody out. My first year, Dallas had just run us out of the stadium (59-14). Then, to come back and beat them so bad, a real good ball club, well, it just did a lot for our confidence.

When we played Dallas in the championship game, I didn't realize until afterwards that we'd turned the ball over five times. That made us [defensive players] feel real good that we'd been able to play so well defensively that we could win even with all those turnovers.

But what I remember most about the championship game is that I got the chicken pox on the Thursday before the game. And when we went back for the Super Bowl, I was still sick. I lost about 12 pounds that week and I missed a lot of practice time.

What I remember most about the Super Bowl is the play I missed. At that time I wasn't playing on every down, and I thought I was supposed to come out of the game when it was third-and-one on our six. But I was supposed to stay in, and when I came out we only had 10 men on the field. Pete Johnson ran right through the spot where I would have been for the first down. It was a darn good thing we stopped them, because otherwise there would have been

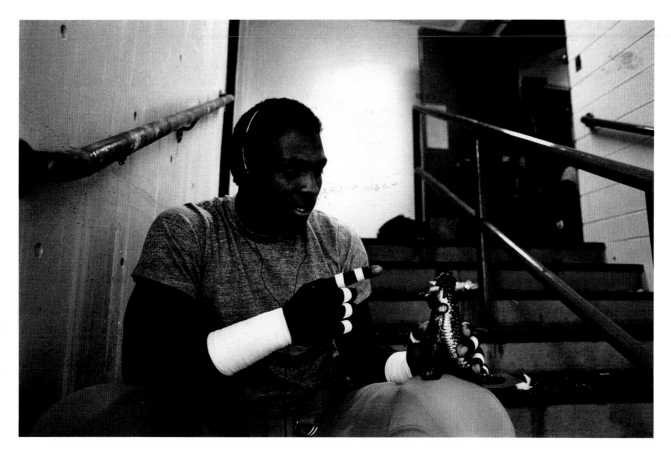

a lot of headlines about me being out of the game on the key play.

In '84 we honestly felt from the beginning that we would win. When we won the Super Bowl it was just what we expected. From the beginning of the season we were talking about that.

Even when Miami came right down and scored we weren't shook up. Danny [Marino] had had a great season and everybody wondered if we'd be able to stop him, but we felt we could. We made the right kind of adjustments, going to a 4-3, and we were OK.

It doesn't seem like I've been playing 10 years. Maybe that's because every year has been different. Every year the team seems to have a different personality. Whether it's injuries or trying to repeat as champions, we always seem to have a different set of obstacles, a different set of questions.

Personally, I've become a lot more comfortable with myself. I've had to learn to deal with periods when I haven't had success, or the team hasn't. Early in my career I used to eat myself alive about not doing well. I'm not saying that I accept it and like it, but at least I've learned to accept it when I don't do as well as I think I should, or if I get hurt, or if the team loses. I think I do a pretty good job of dealing with it now.

I used to worry about not getting enough credit for what I was doing. I've always taken pride in doing everything well, but this is the age of the specialist. Guys get credit for just doing one thing, when that may be all they do. I understand that now.

Early in my career I was hung up on the idea of having to get better each year. I don't know whether that's happened. I'm really not in the best position to judge that, or what year has been my best. The important thing is whether the team wins, and the Super Bowl years have been best because of that.

To be involved in three Super Bowls has been a real thrill. I've come to expect that we should win.

A lot of our success should be credited to our owner, Eddie DeBartolo. We've had very few [money] problems compared to other teams. I know from talking to players on other teams how good we've had it here.

When teams have problems it always stems from a lack of communication. Not just between owner and players or coaches and players, but even players and players.

Bill Walsh should take credit for putting together a team with players who can work together. It's not necessarily that we all like each other, but we have a focus. We have common goals.

I honestly think that's the most important thing, because in football you have to rely on so many people. You look out on the field and see 11 players, but it goes beyond that. Special teams are very important, for instance. We have the feeling that everybody on the team is important. Everybody makes a contribution in one way or another. There's no way you can just be here and not do anything.

Bill has done a good job. I don't judge a coach just on his game plan, although that's important, but on the way he puts the players together, and Bill has been able to get the right kind of players.

Roger Craig

Sheer determination, as well as talent, have made Roger Craig the most dangerous all-purpose back in the NFL.

Nobody trains harder than Roger in the off-season — he is working on a book on his conditioning program, Turn It Up Another Notch — and his willingness to work turned him from a back who seldom caught a pass in college to one who is the best all-purpose back in the NFL.

In 1985 Craig became the only player in NFL history to gain more than 1,000 yards both rushing and receiving — 1,050 yards rushing and 1,016 receiving. His combined yardage of 2,066 was a team record, and his 92 receptions were a league record for running back. He was honored by his teammates as winner of the Len Eshmont Award for the most "courageous and inspirational player" that season.

In the 1985 Super Bowl he set game records for points (18) and touchdowns (3) and accounted for 135 yards rushing and receiving.

In the 1988 season Craig led the National Conference in rushing with 1,502 yards.

Craig donates time to numerous charitable organizations in the off-season and has also modeled for Macy's.

■ When I was at Nebraska I talked to pro scouts who told me that it was important to be able to catch passes, so when we had winter conditioning programs I'd work with the wide receivers and catch maybe 100 balls a day. Since I've been with the 49ers I've worked with receivers like Fred Solomon and Dwight Clark, who have really taught me a lot. They taught me how a receiver thinks — not just catching the ball but being prepared to run with it after I caught it.

I think what really opened the 49ers' eyes was the first mini-camp after I was drafted in '83. Paul Hackett was the quarterback coach then and he threw me about 80 passes; I think I only dropped about three. That showed them what a good receiver I could be.

One thing I remember before I was drafted: I met Riki Ellison, who's been a good friend ever since, at the combine meeting [at which top college seniors meet and work out together before the draft]. Gil Brandt of Dallas told us he didn't think we could play, Riki because he'd had operations on his knee, and me because I couldn't catch the ball. So when we beat Dallas in the final game of the '83 season Riki and I got a special satisfaction out of it.

It was a big adjustment for me to make when I came here. I wasn't a true fullback. I'd played tailback for three years in college and then was shifted to fullback my senior year. I wasn't really comfortable there because I wasn't the big, bruising fullback type.

But at the time I came here the 49ers had just traded for Wendell Tyler, and he was the big gun. I had to block for Wendell, to make the holes for him. I really banged up my shoulders. I took a real pounding. But I knew this was the best thing for the team and that my time to be the major ballcarrier would come.

We had a pretty good thing going, too. Teams had to key on Wendell running the ball, so that left me free to catch passes. The 1,000-1,000 [rushing and receiving] year, we could have been one of only about three or four teams in history to have two runners with 1,000 yards. Wendell was on his way to that when he hurt his knee.

I knew I was going to have a great season. I was just taking up where I'd left off in the Super Bowl. That was the game that really got me national visibility. I think it was the first time that a lot of people really knew about me. I had gone into that game thinking I really wanted to play as hard as I could and do as well as I could because I couldn't be sure that I'd ever be in another Super Bowl.

I didn't have any goals that next season, but when I got to about 800-800 it became a realistic thing for me to think about 1,000-1,000. From that point on I heard about it from everybody — coaches, writers. Everybody was wondering if I could make it. I really had to bang myself up to make it, but it's something I'll cherish for the rest of my life, knowing that I was the first one to do it.

But really, last year was probably more satisfying because I was really the dominating player, the franchise player, the guy who the team expected to get the job done. I had a lot of help, with big Tom Rathman opening up the holes for me. But this gave me the chance to really show my talent.

In the same way, the whole year was more satisfying for both me and the team than the '84 season. That year we really expected to win. Then, when we got to the Super Bowl, we had the best record in the league and so much depth that we just assumed we'd win, and we did.

But last season was really gratifying because we had so much adversity. We had a lot of injuries, and then Joe [Montana] and Steve [Young] were going back and forth at quarterback, so we didn't know what was happening. And we had a young group of guys who didn't really know what it took to win. Guys like Jerry Rice, Harris Barton — they're really young. They didn't know how to turn it up another notch.

So it was up to guys like Randy Cross, myself, and Keena Turner to call meetings and remind them to keep their minds on the game. We reminded them what we could do if we played together.

We pulled the team together, got the family feeling back. For a couple of years we'd lost that. The chemistry wasn't there. The love wasn't there. But we found the love last year to pull the team together.

Bill [Walsh] put all the distractions behind him, too. He was like an old boxer, going back to his roots to find out who he was. He had the eye of the tiger going down the stretch. He was just doing whatever it took to win.

Then, to get back to the Super Bowl — that was really exciting, knowing that millions of people would be watching us again. The two weeks leading up to the game are exciting because the fans are all involved and the media is all there. I love all the hype.

The game itself was exciting because Sam Wyche was the Cincinnati coach and he'd been an assistant for us. It was teacher versus pupil, and the teacher showed he was better. I guess you can never beat the teacher. You can't beat that experience.

When we started that last drive we were really calm because we had practiced that situation all year. Joe just marched us down the field. He'd throw a swing pass to me and out pass to Jerry. Whatever it took, that's what we did. It was like a dream come true.

My whole 49er career has been very gratifying. I've worked very hard to keep it going because I've never wanted to be in the position after my career is over to say that I could have done even more if I'd just worked a little harder.

I'll never be content, never be satisfied that I've done everything I can do. I think that attitude is important whatever you're doing. I think you can be successful in any field if you've got the right attitude.

I'm always happy, always upbeat. Life is too short to get down on yourself.

Postgame

RIGHT: *January 8, 1984; NFC Championship; RFK Stadium, Washington, DC. Dwight Hicks speaks to his teammates, telling them to "remember this feeling...remember how this feels...so it will never happen to us again." The 49ers lost to the Washington Redskins 24-21 in a game marred by two late-drive penalties.*
BELOW: *September 23, 1984; Veterans Stadium, Philadelphia. In the City of Brotherly Love, Larry "Pooba-Bear" Pillers and Dwaine "Pee Wee" Board whoop it up with Gandor and Bemular (son of Godzilla). Bemular traveled with the team throughout the season.*
RIGHT: *December 16, 1979; Fulton County Stadium, Atlanta. O.J. Simpson, the ball from his final carry firmly in his hand, heads down the tunnel to the locker room for the last time.* PREVIOUS PAGE, LEFT: *October 21, 1979; Candlestick Park. Assistant coach Mike White embraces his close friend Bill Walsh after Walsh's first league win, 20-15, over the Atlanta Falcons.* PREVIOUS PAGE, RIGHT: *December 11, 1988; Candlestick Park. His back a mass of welts accumulated from a season's worth of hits, Roger Craig queues up with his teammates for a postgame shave.*

September 4, 1988; Superdome, New Orleans. Bill Walsh addresses the team moments after the opening-game victory over a tough New Orleans team. After congratulating the team, he reminds them to be back in Santa Clara the next morning, ready to prepare for the New York Giants. Tuesday is the players' day off. LEFT: *January 1, 1989; NFC Divisional Playoff; Candlestick Park. A jovial Joe Montana and Bill Walsh ham it up in the waning moments of the 49er 34-9 victory over the Minnesota Vikings.*

January 1, 1989; NFC Divisional Playoff; Candlestick Park. Joe Montana, who rarely addresses the team in a postgame locker room, awards the game ball to coach Walsh in honor of his 100th victory. The 49ers won 34-9. BELOW: *November 2, 1980; Pontiac, Michigan. Edward DeBartolo, Jr., and his father, Edward De Bartolo, Sr., are grim after a heartbreaking 17-13 loss to Detroit. One year later they would return to the same stadium to celebrate a Super Bowl victory.*

January 24, 1982; Super Bowl XVI; Pontiac, Michigan. A jubilant 49er team meets with CBS announcer Brent Musburger after their victory. Left to right, Charle Young, Dan Bunz (holding the Super Bowl trophy), Musburger, Hacksaw Reynolds, Bill Walsh, Dwight Clark, Freddie Solomon, Joe Montana, and Edward DeBartolo, Jr.

SUPER BOWL TEAMS

Super Bowl XVI team and coaches (left to right): Al Vermeil, Bill McPherson, Cas Banaszek, George Seifert, Milt Jackson, Bill Walsh, Chuck Studley, Sam Wyche, Norb Hecker, Bobb McKittrick, Ray Rhodes, Billie Mathews.

Super Bowl XIX team and coaches (left to right): Bill Walsh, Tommy Hart, Bill McPherson, Jerry Attaway, Fred vonAppen, Ray Rhodes. Bottom row: Norb Hecker, George Seifert, Bobb McKittrick, Paul Hackett, Sherman Lewis.

Super Bowl XXIII team and coaches (left to right): Bill Walsh, Denny Green, Jerry Attaway, Tommy Hart, Bill McPherson, Mike Holmgren. Bottom row: Fred vonAppen, Lynn Stiles, Ray Rhodes, Sherman Lewis, Bobb McKittrick, George Seifert.

RIGHT: *December 1, 1985; RFK Stadium, Washington, DC. Joe Montana unloads to Jerry Rice as the 49ers blast the Redskins 35-8 on Monday night.*

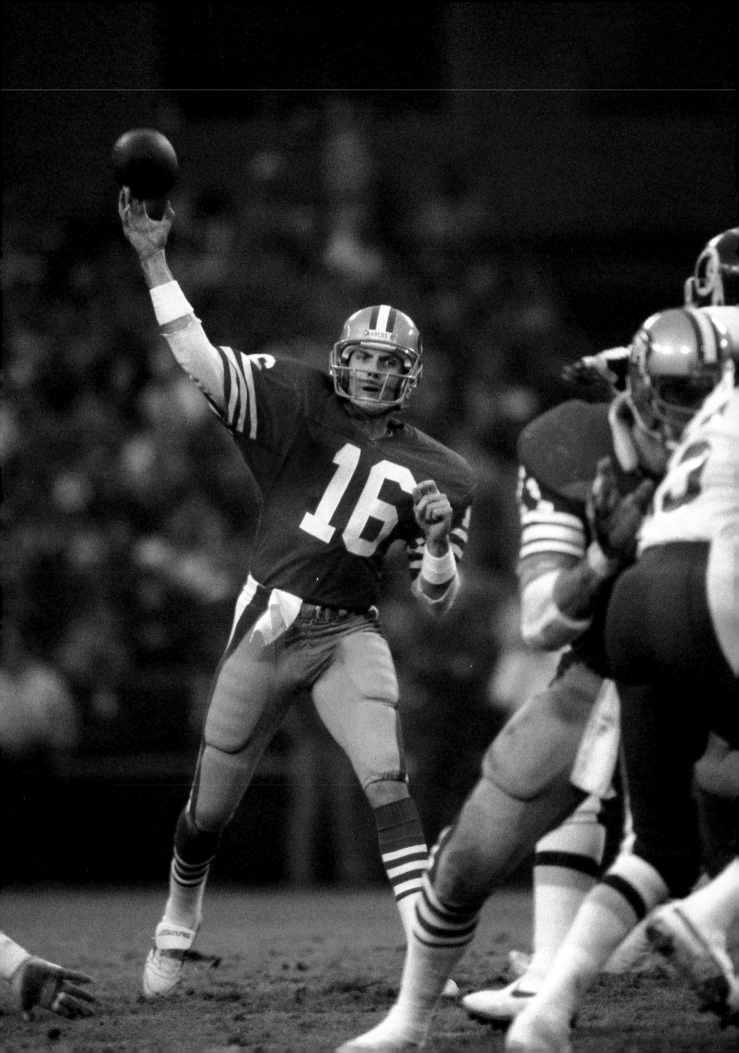

ABOVE: *September 4, 1988; Superdome, New Orleans. Joe Montana calling an audible in a crucial third-down play. The 49ers outlasted the Saints 34-33.*
RIGHT: *September 2, 1984; Silverdome, Pontiac, Michigan. Ray Wersching boots the game-winning field goal as the 49ers defeat Detroit 30-27 in the season opener. Joe Montana always held the ball for Mo. Danny Bunz holds off two Lions.* FAR RIGHT: *August 18, 1984; Jack Murphy Stadium, San Diego. Larry Pillers and Keena Turner pile-drive Chuck Muncie into the infield dirt in a preseason clash.*

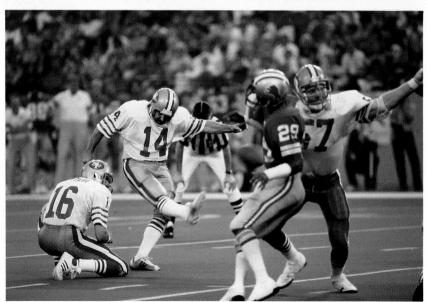

NEXT SUNDAY, THE 49ERS WILL BE IN
PITTSBURGH TO TANGLE WITH THE
STEELERS...YOU CAN
CATCH ALL THE ACTION ON KCBS 740
RADIO OR KPIX TV, CHANNEL 5...
CHECK YOUR LOCAL LISTINGS & ROOT!!

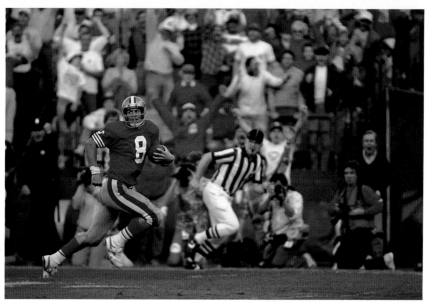

ABOVE: *October 25, 1981; Candlestick Park. Joe Montana scrambles down to the one-yard line as the 49ers beat Los Angeles at home in one of the big wins of 1981.* LEFT: *October 30, 1988; Candlestick Park. Looking back over his shoulder, Steve Young races for the end zone, stunning Minnesota with a last-minute 49-yard run.* FAR LEFT: *August 27, 1987; Candlestick Park. Tom Rathman leaps over fallen blocker Jesse Sapolu in a preseason clash with San Diego.*

July 31, 1988; Wembley Stadium, London. Roger Craig is flipped skyward by a host of Dolphin defenders. BELOW: *August 23, 1986; Mile High Stadium, Denver. Denver Bronco back caught in a savage pincer between Jeff Fuller and Ronnie Lott in a preseason game.* PREVIOUS PAGE, LEFT: *September 22, 1985; Memorial Coliseum, Los Angeles. Eric Wright bats a pass away from Jessie Hester at the last second, helping the 49ers to defeat the Raiders.* PREVIOUS PAGE, RIGHT: *December 22, 1985; Candlestick Park. Keith Fahnhorst acts as convoy for Roger Craig as Craig goes over the 1000-1000 mark. The 49ers beat Dallas 31-16 to gain a wild card slot in the play-offs.*

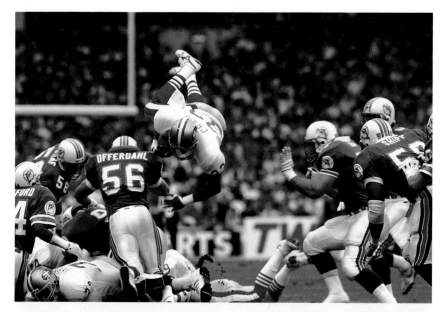

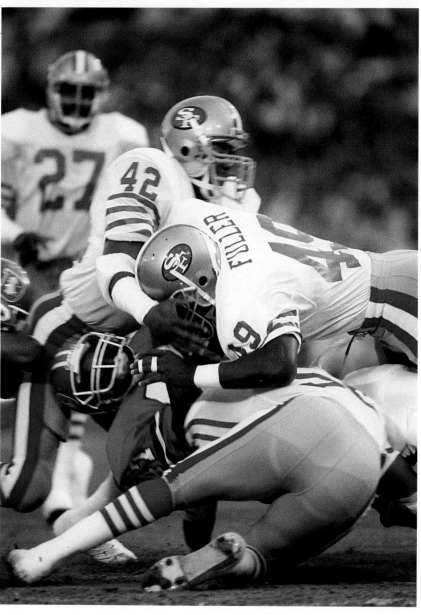

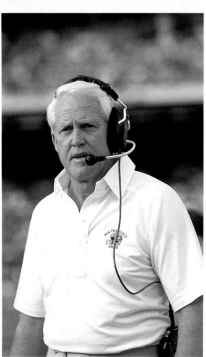

December 1, 1985; RFK Stadium, Washington, DC. Wendell Tyler is up-ended as he vaults into the end zone to score a touchdown in the 49ers' 35-8 Monday night win over the Redskins. This was Tyler's last season at full strength. BELOW: *November 1, 1987; Anaheim. Head coach Bill Walsh surveys the action as the 49ers trounce the Rams 31-10. In nine years of playing the Rams, Bill led the 49ers to seven wins.*

December 29, 1984; NFC Divisional Playoff; Candlestick Park. Joe Montana sets to throw behind a phalanx of blockers—Fred Quillan (56), John Ayers (68), and Bubba Paris (77). BELOW: *April 1986; Redwood City. Forty Niner general manager John McVay scans the field during the 49ers' spring mini-camp.* FAR RIGHT: *December 1, 1986; Candlestick Park. Michael Carter manhandles New York Giant back Joe Morris as Mike Walter comes up to help in what proved to be a 21-17 loss to the soon-to-be Super Bowl champs.*

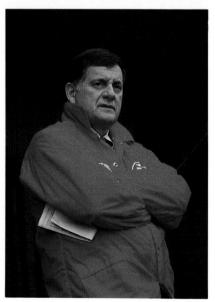

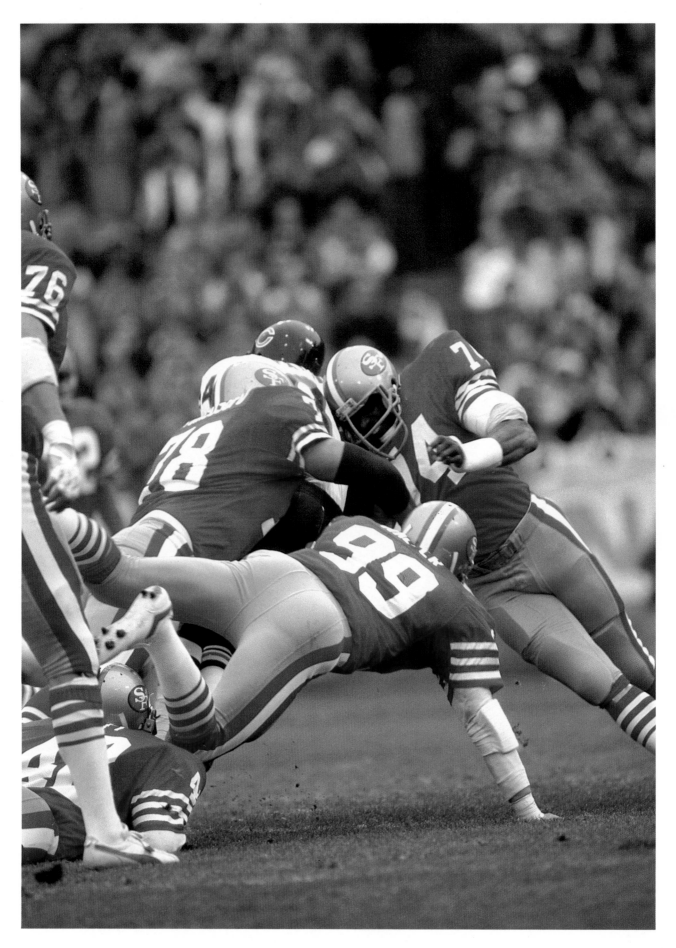

January 22, 1989; Super Bowl XXIII; Joe Robbie Stadium, Miami. Jerry Rice explodes into the Cincinnati secondary with his last and possibly biggest reception of the day in the waning moments of the last 49er drive. LEFT: *December 21, 1980; Candlestick Park. In the mire of the mud, the 49ers drop their final season game to the Buffalo Bills.* FAR LEFT: *January 6, 1985; NFC Championship; Candlestick Park. Fred Dean, Manu Tuiasosopo, and Mike Walter slam Walter Payton to the turf as the 49ers up-end the Monsters of the Midway to earn their second Super Bowl trip in four years.*

January 22, 1989; Super Bowl XXIII; Joe Robbie Stadium, Miami. Pandemonium reigns in the 49er locker room moments after a game many consider the best Super Bowl ever. PREVIOUS PAGE, LEFT: *November 23, 1986; Candlestick Park. Rookie cornerback Don Griffin comes up to make the play on Atlanta wide receiver Charlie Brown.* PREVIOUS PAGE, RIGHT: *January 22, 1989; Super Bowl XXIII; Joe Robbie Stadium, Miami. Clutching the pigskin like gold, John Taylor dances into the end zone with only seconds left on the clock, scoring the winning touchdown.*